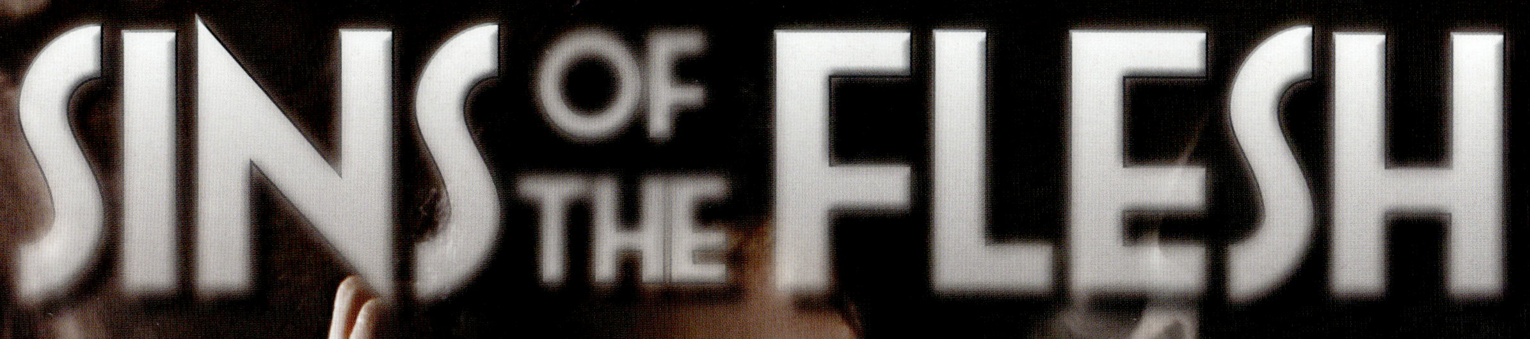

BY BRUCE COLERO

AN SQP PRESENTATION

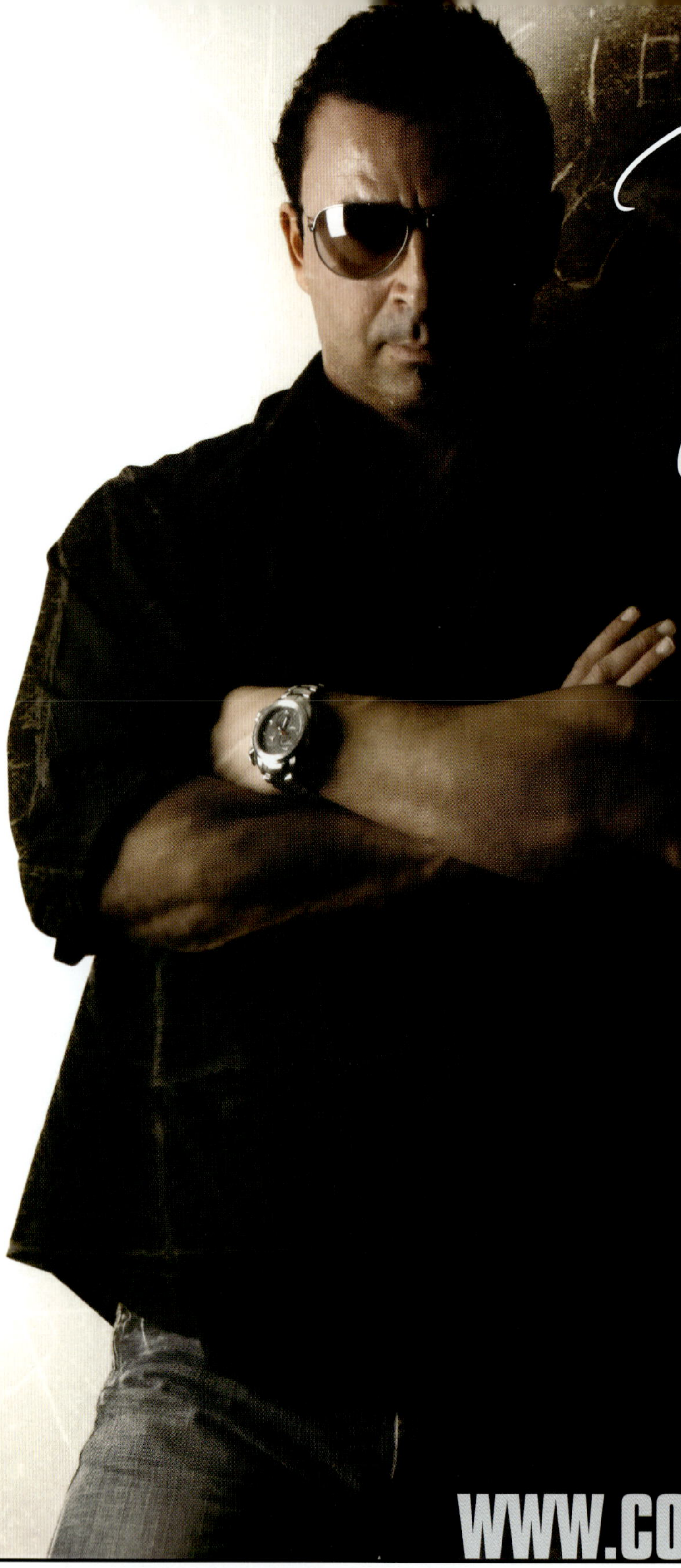

Welcome... to the Dark Side

I've worked with the very elite - from adult film stars like Jesse Jane, Stormy Daniels and Alektra Blue to top ranked centerfolds and Playboy® models like Kobe Kaige, Jenny Poussin and Veronica Zemanova.

My prints, books and posters are sold worldwide and have graced the walls of celebs and athletes alike.

I won't shoot fashion, headshots, or glam.
I won't paint landscapes, portraits, or still lifes...
what I will do...
will blow your mind.

I have to say - the biggest thrill I get from this gig is all the love I get from my fans. The emails, the sexy photos (you naughty girls you) and words of praise - make it all worth it.

You fuckers rock!

Colero

Bruce Colero
November 2012

WWW.COLERO.CA

Sins of the Flesh By Bruce Colero

Book design by Grassy Knoll Studios.

Published by SQP Inc.
PO Box 248 - Columbus NJ 08022

Sal Quartuccio & Bob Keenan - Publishers

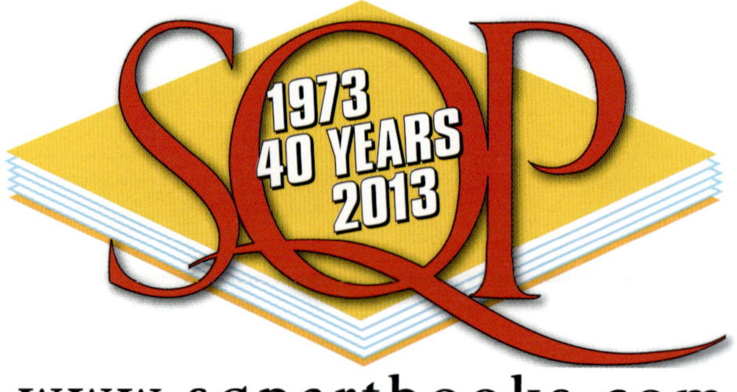

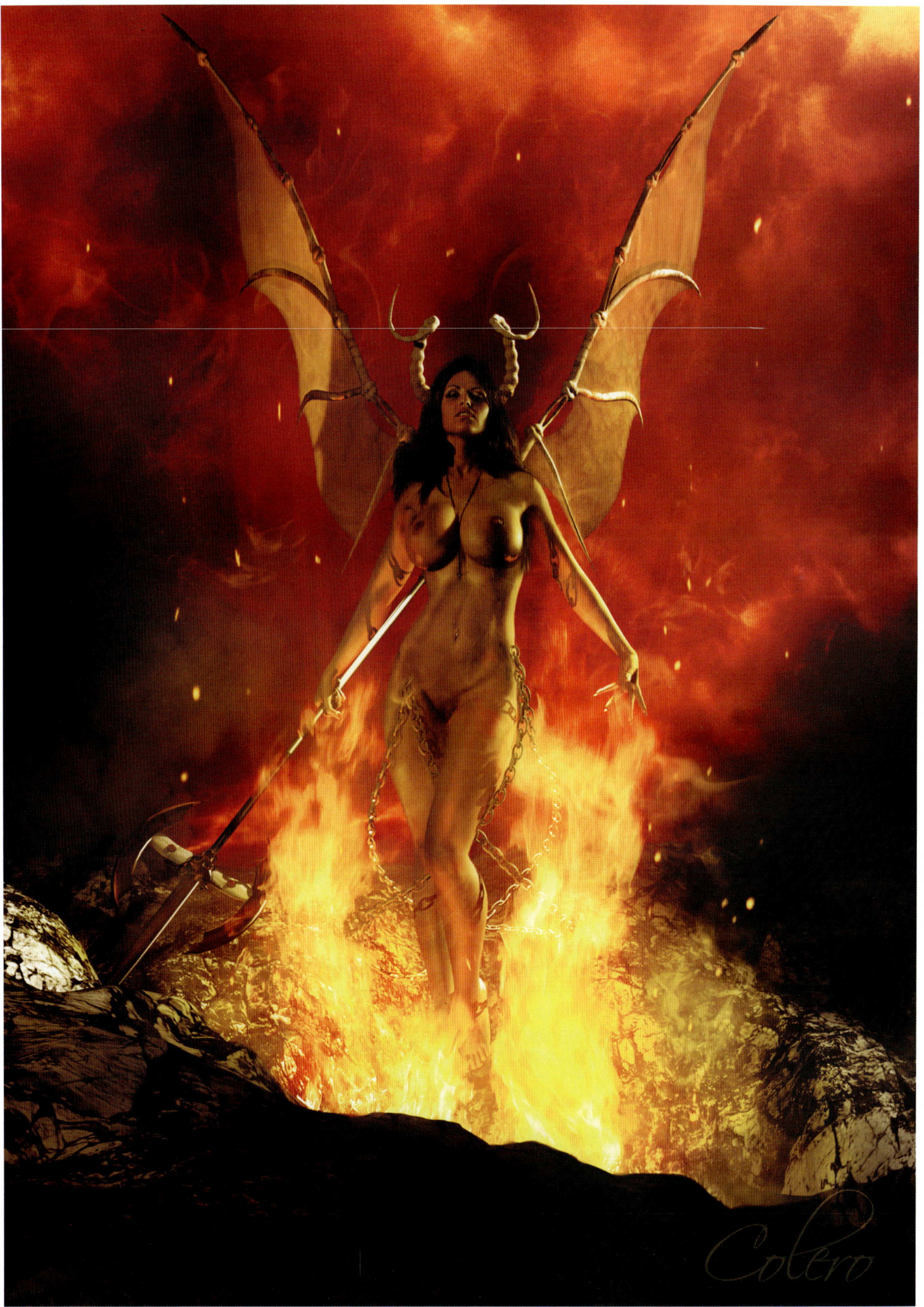

Hell Hath No Fury

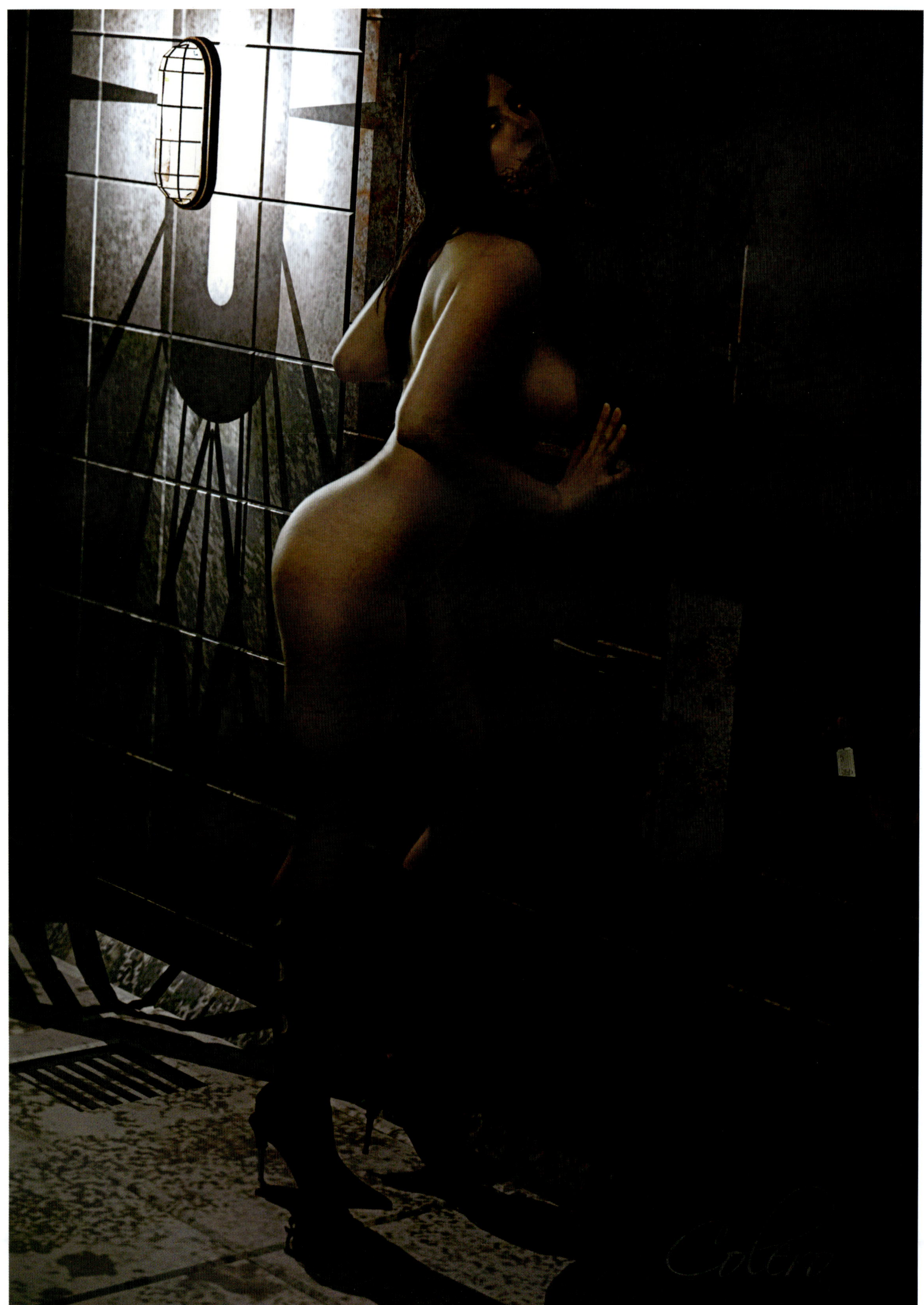

Strigoi

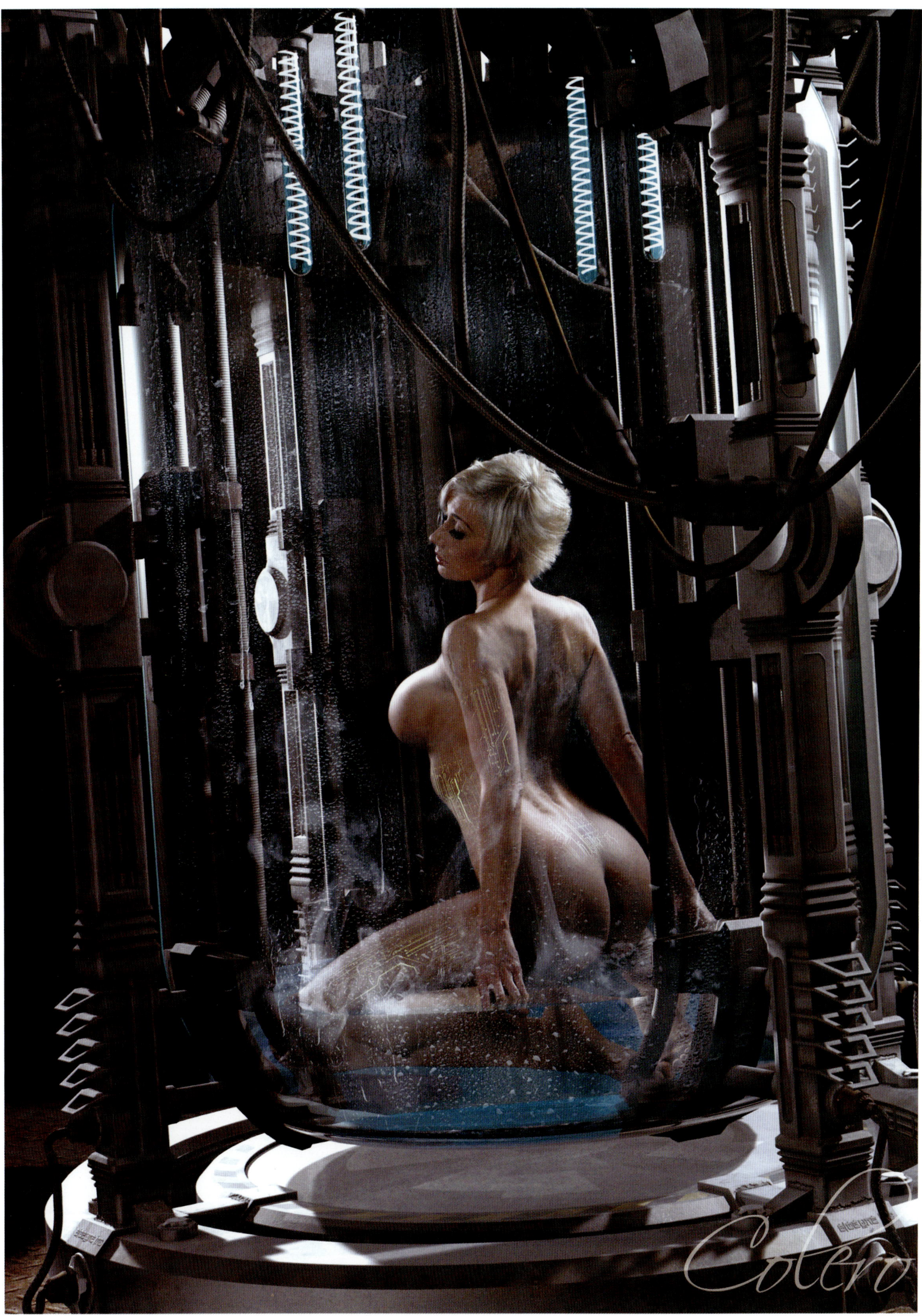

Made in Japan

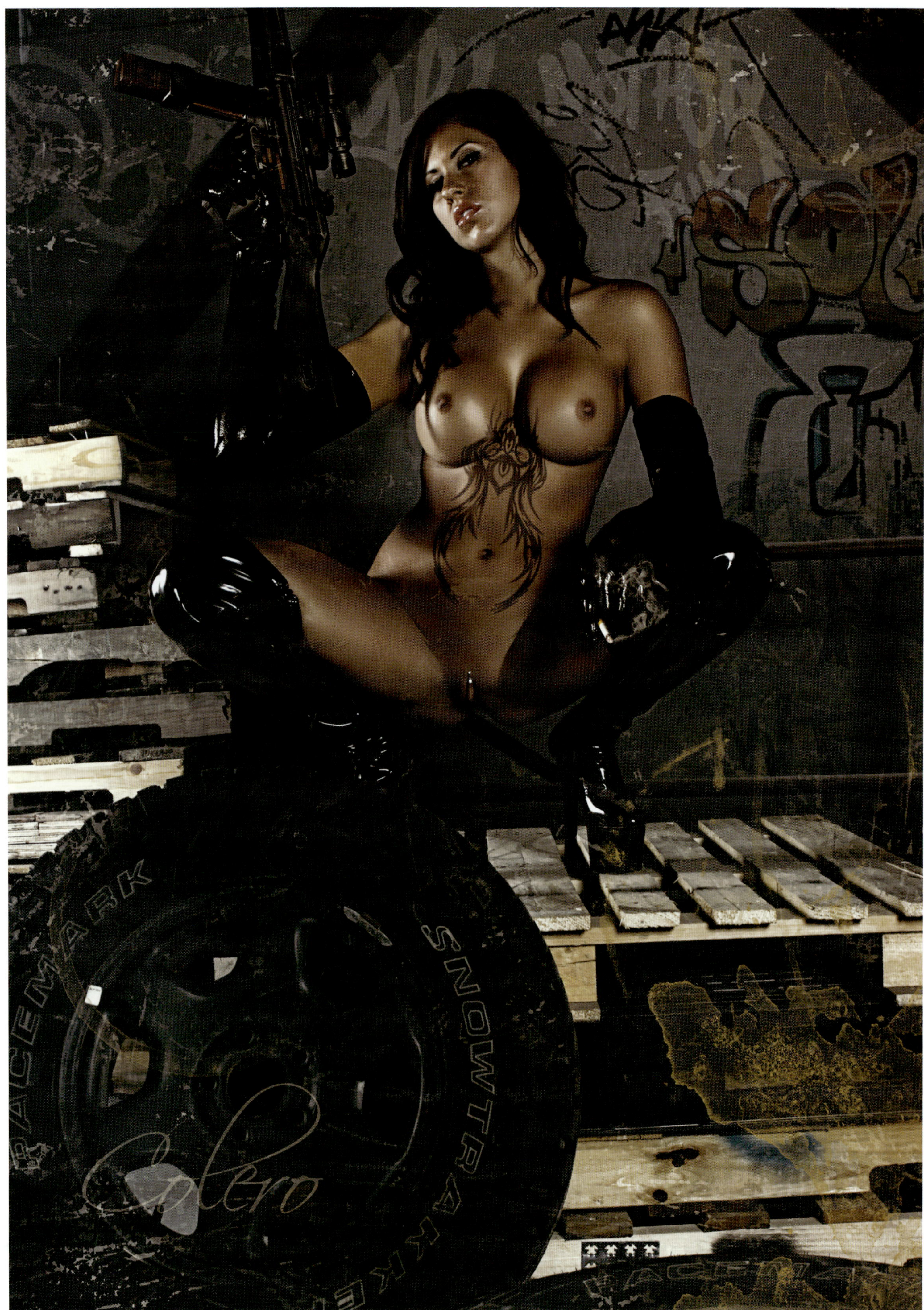

Black Russian

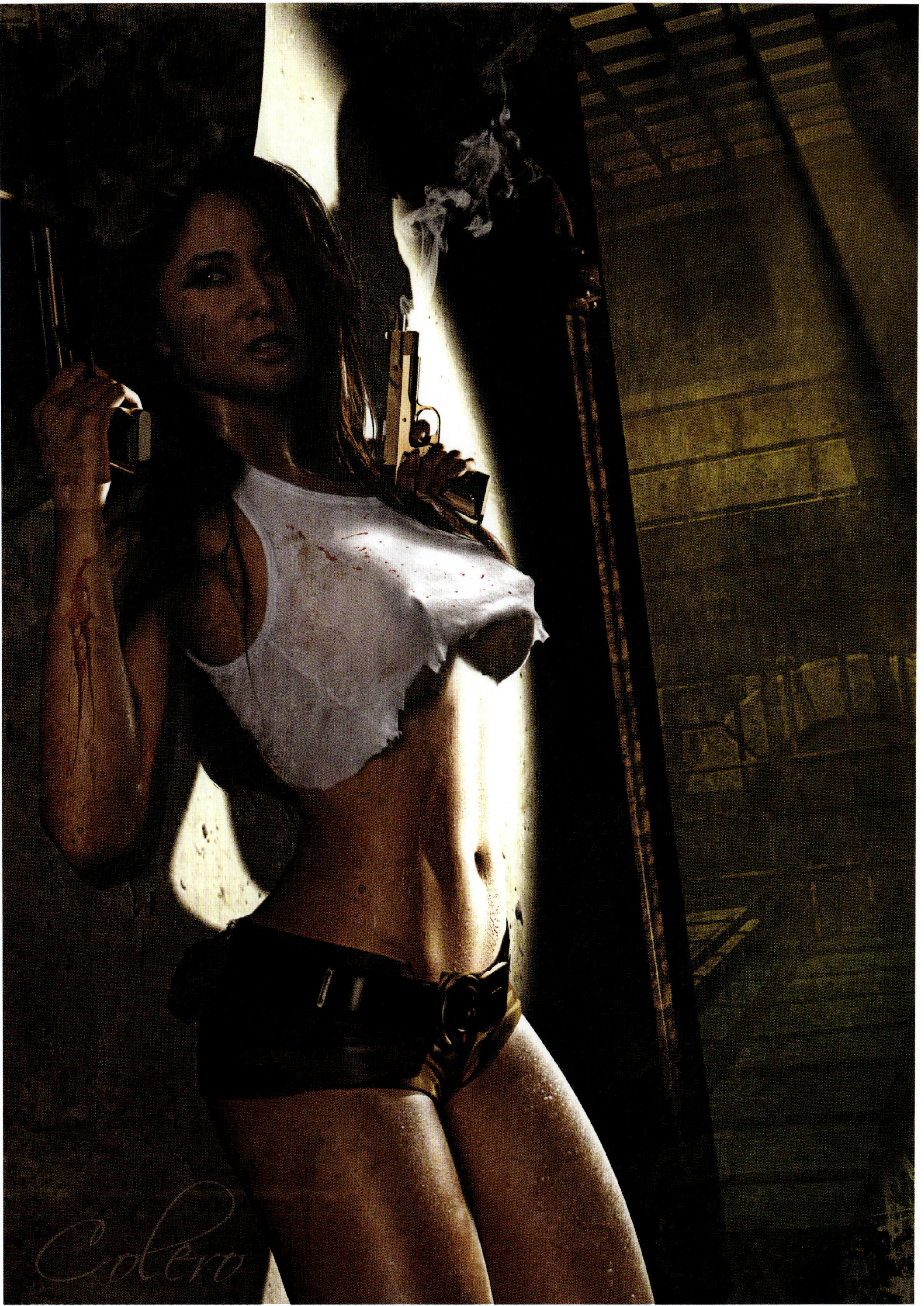

Fear Kills

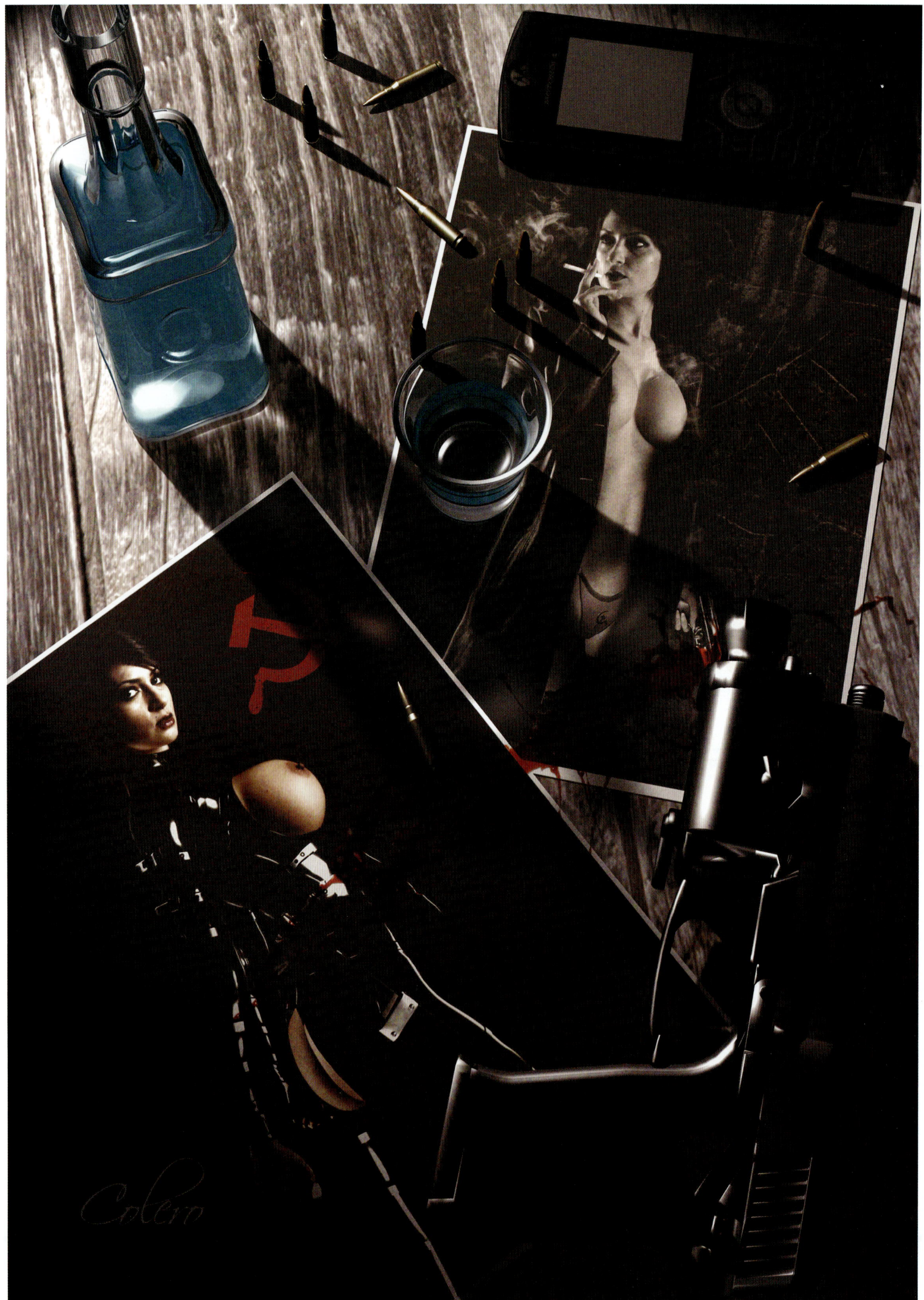

I Spy

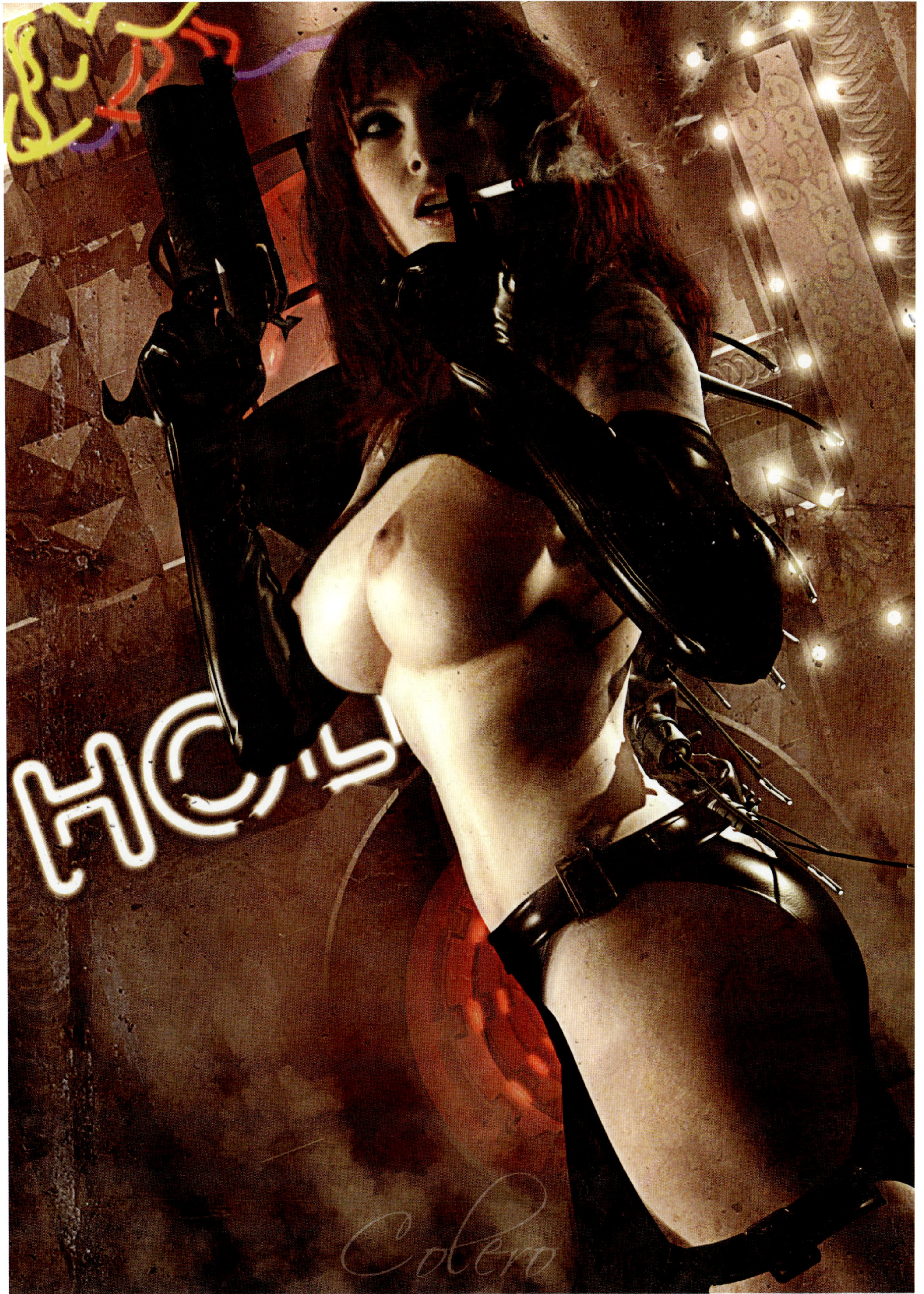

Days of Future Past

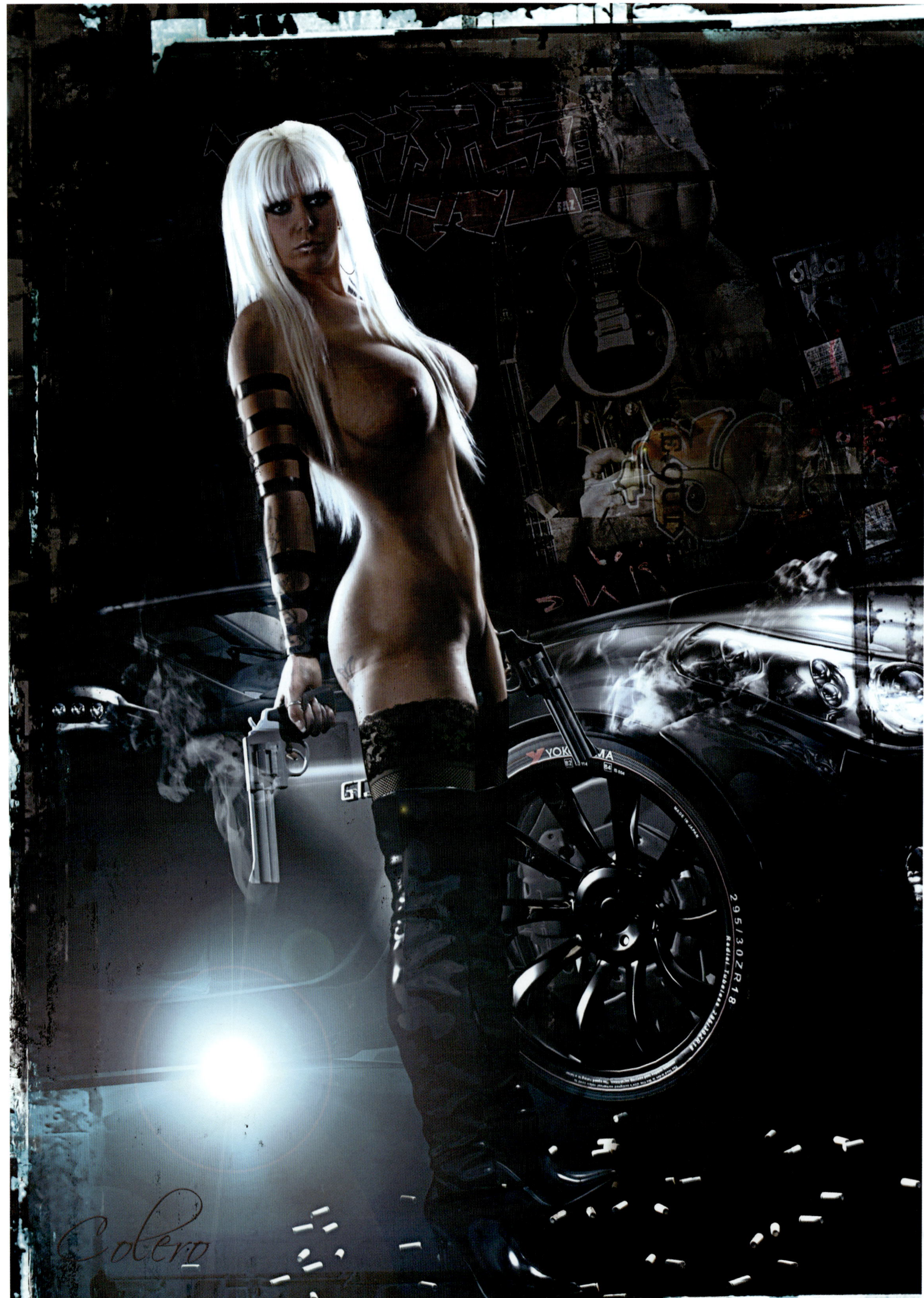

Good at Bad

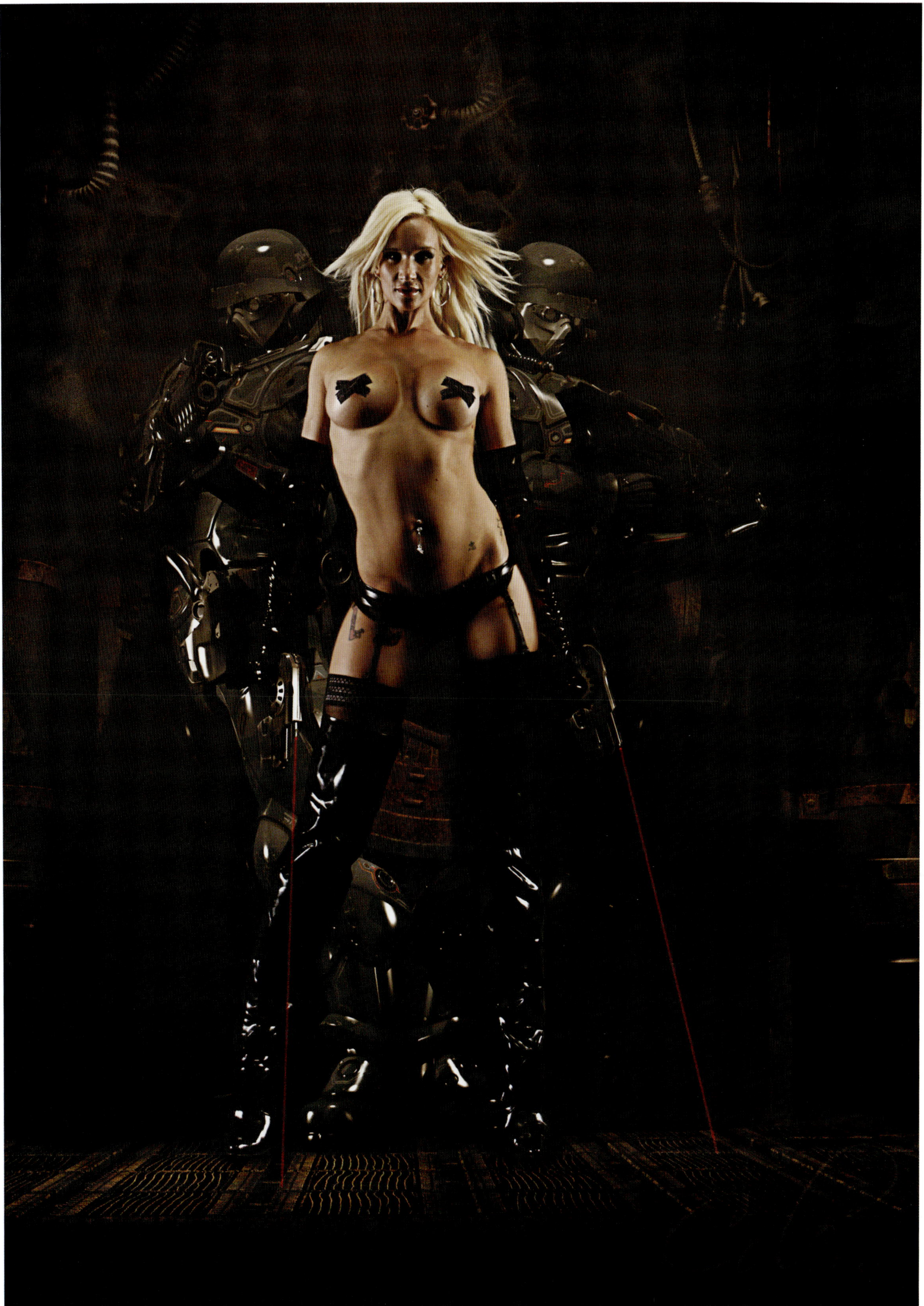

Heavy Metal

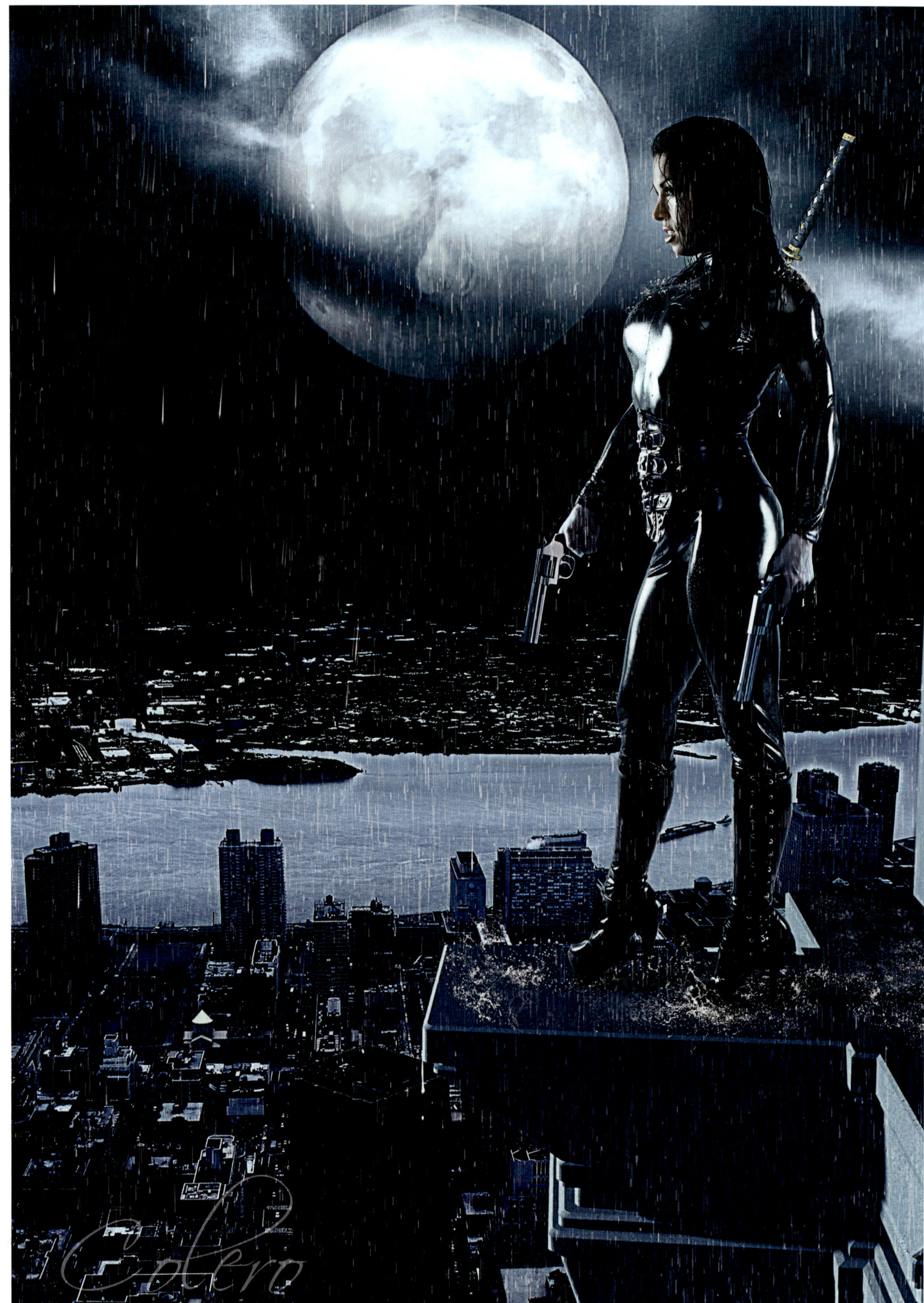

Vanguard

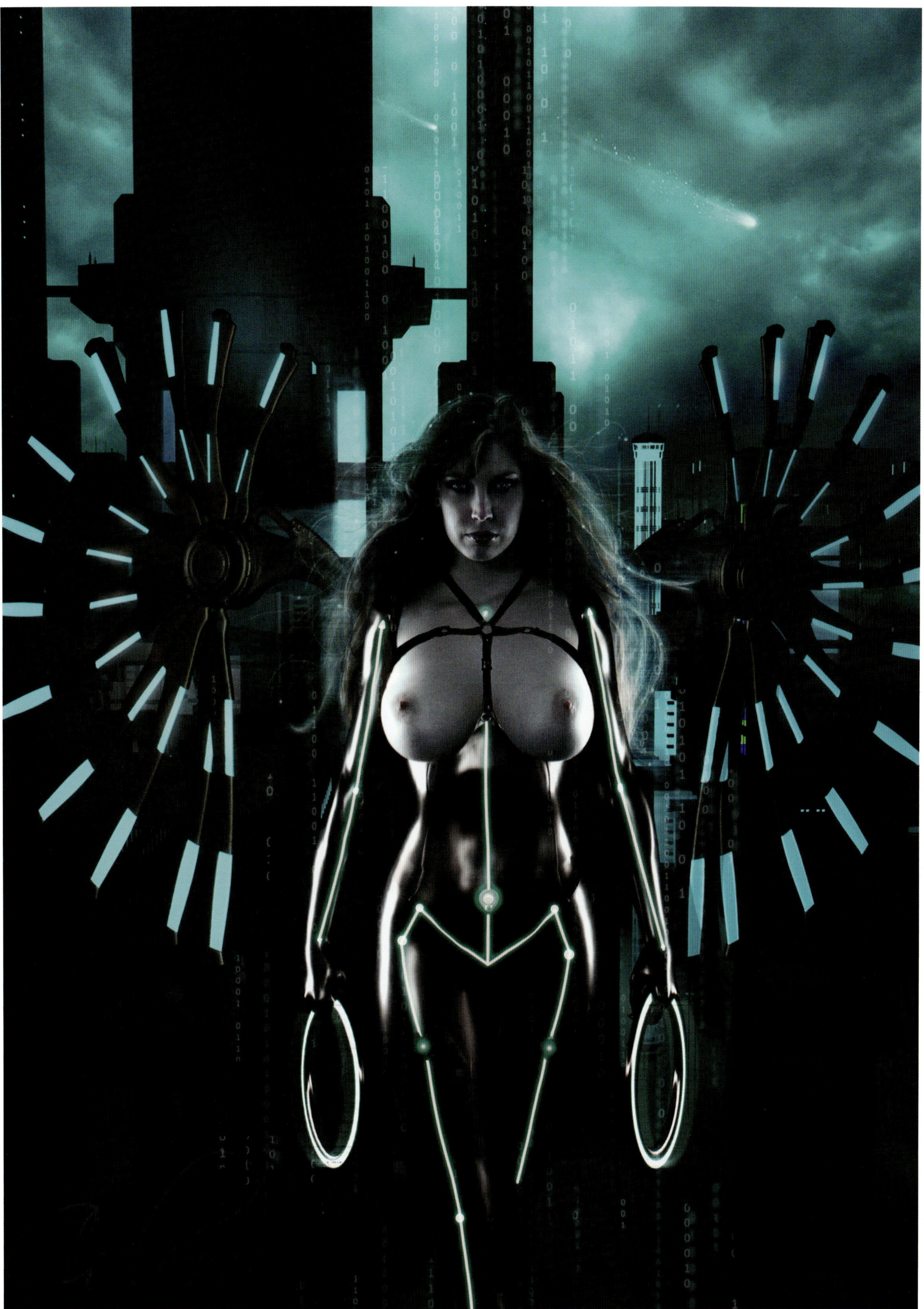

Viral

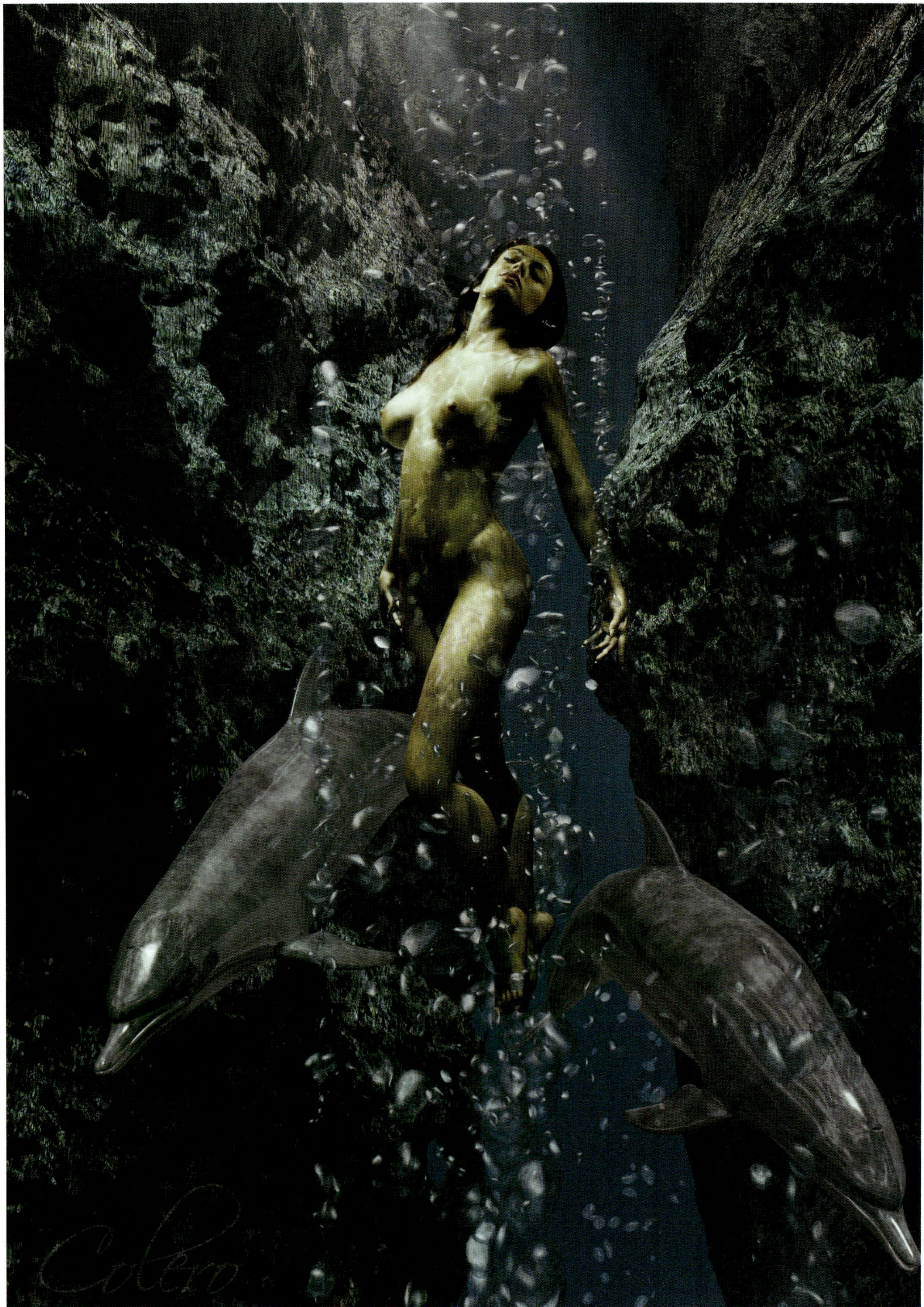

Echo

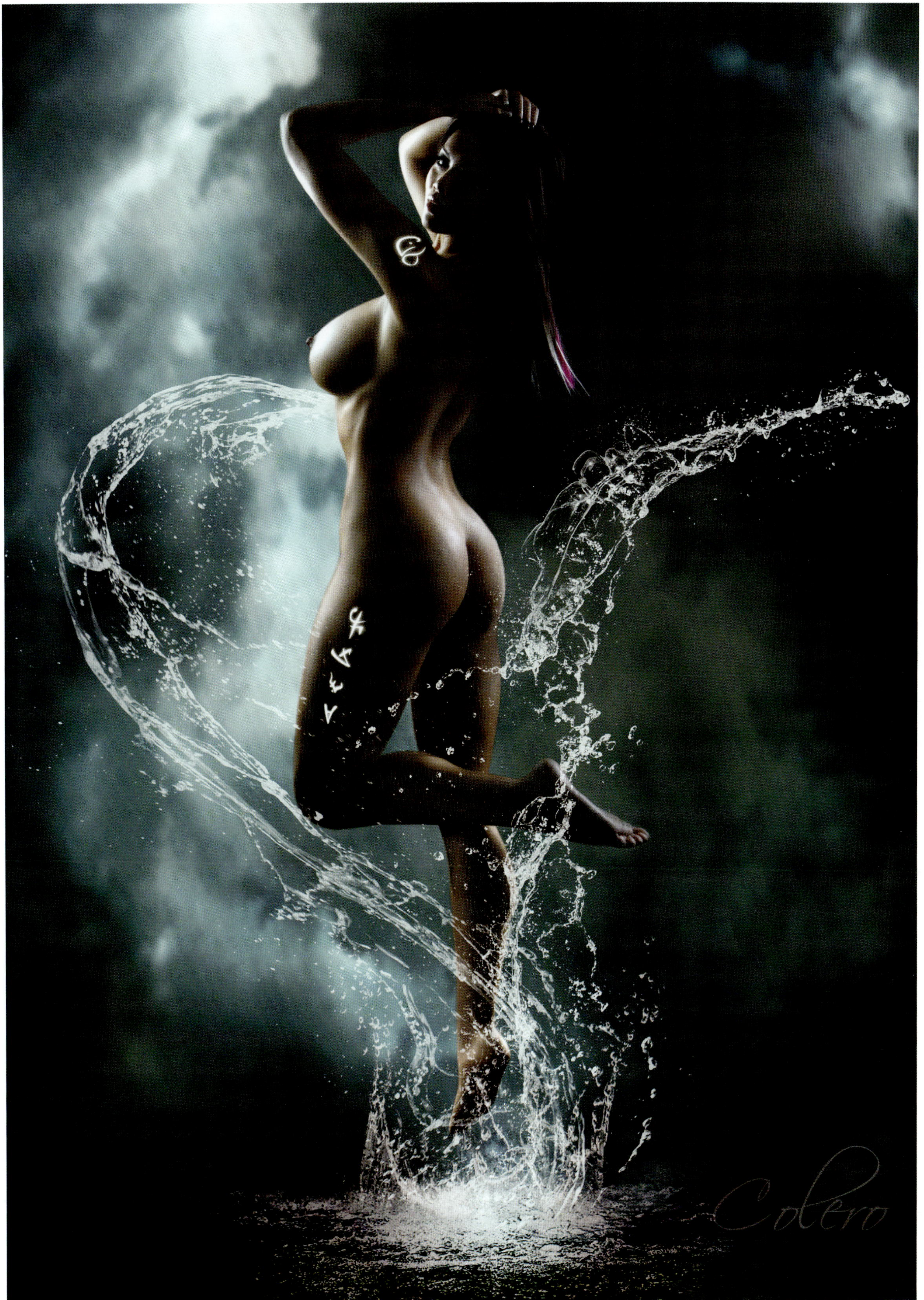

Fathom

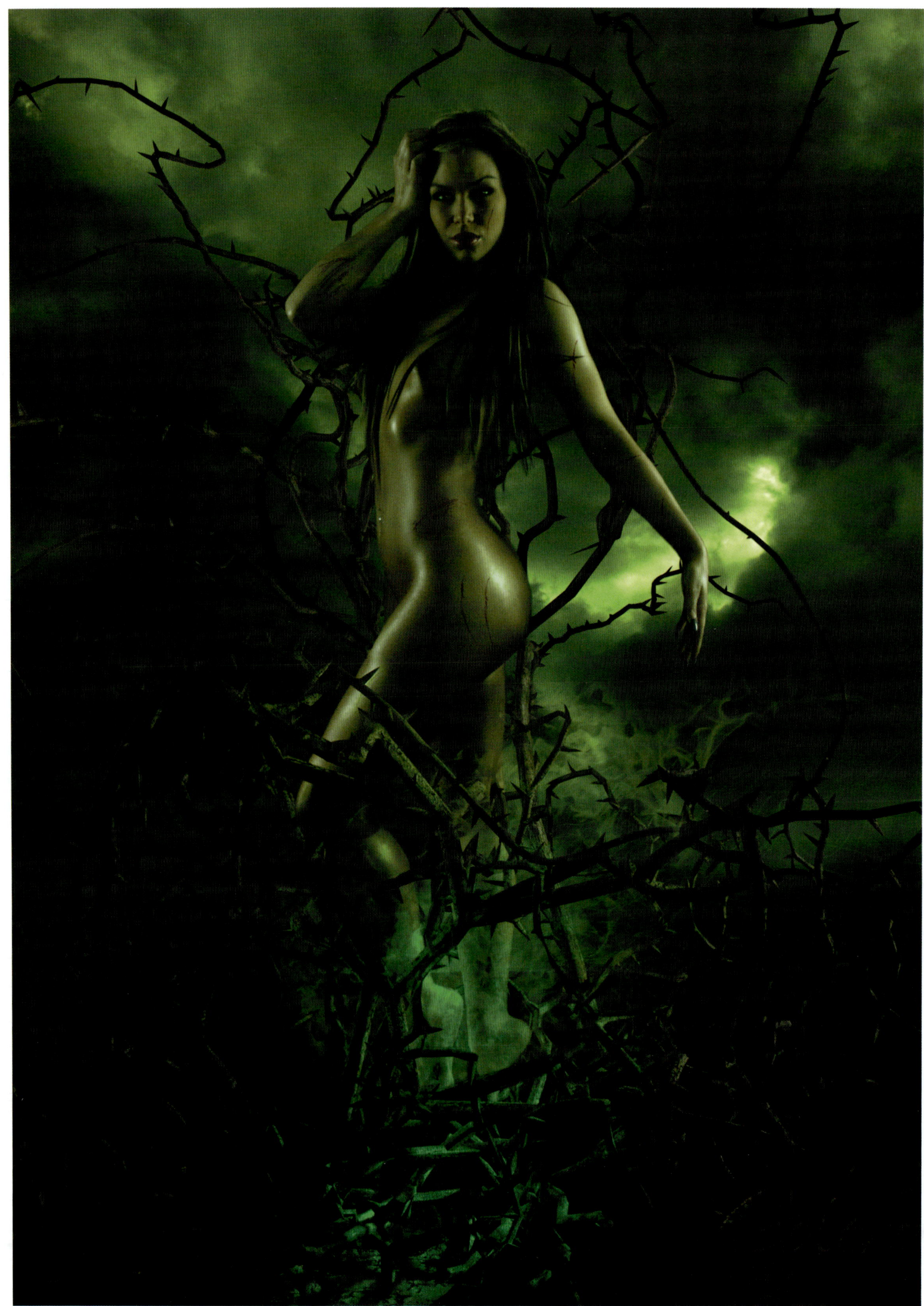

Queen of Thorns

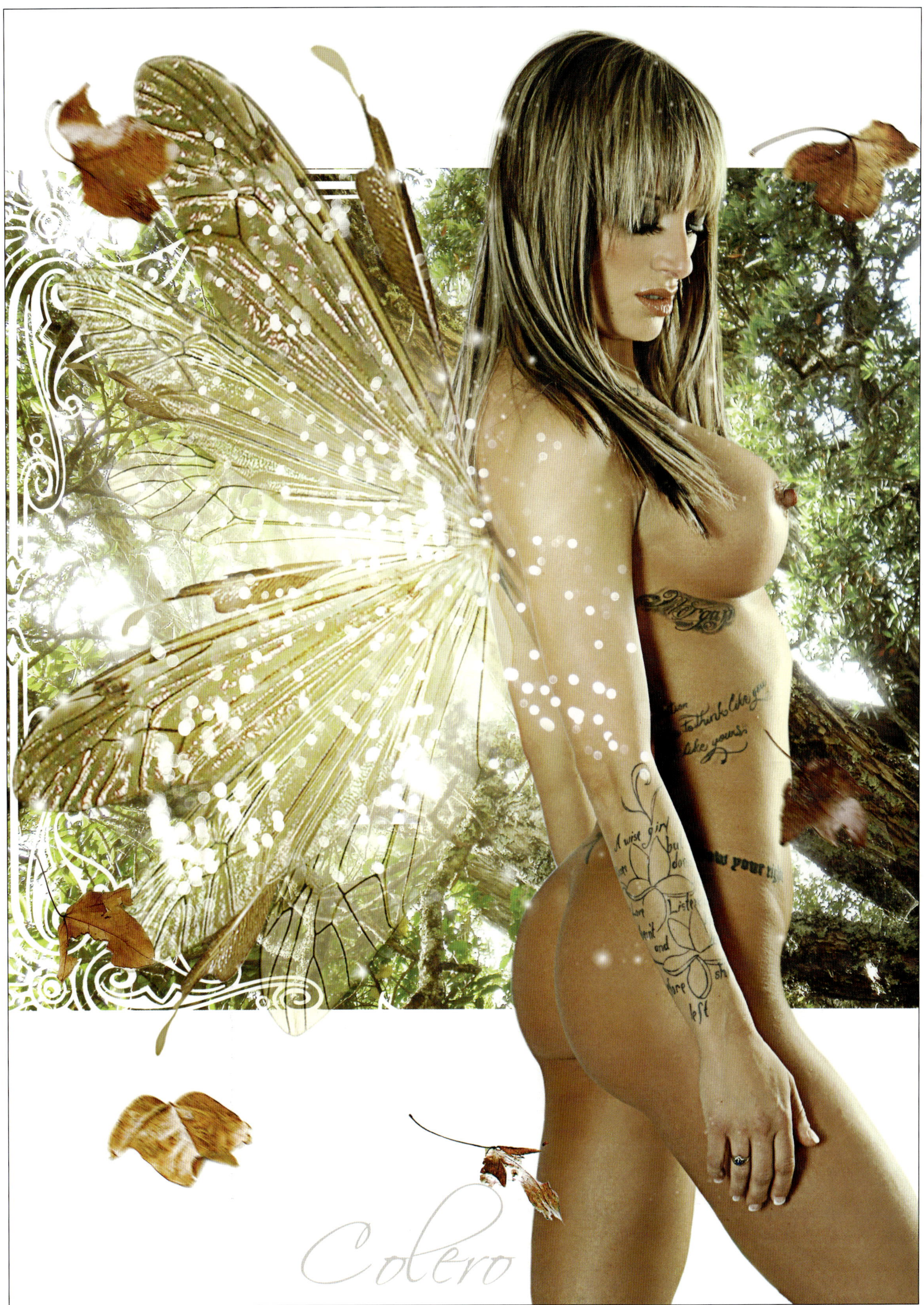

Fae

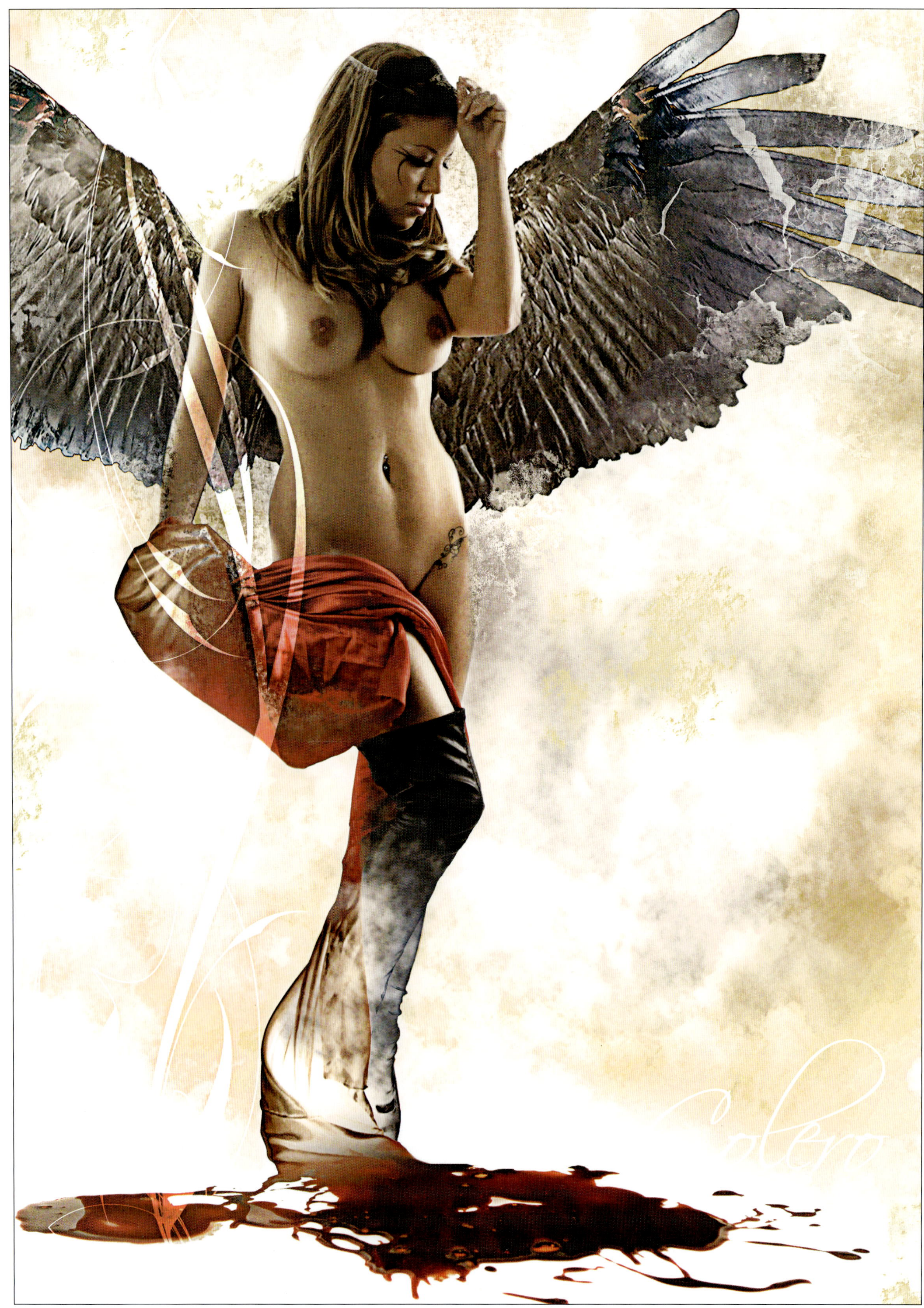

Nike

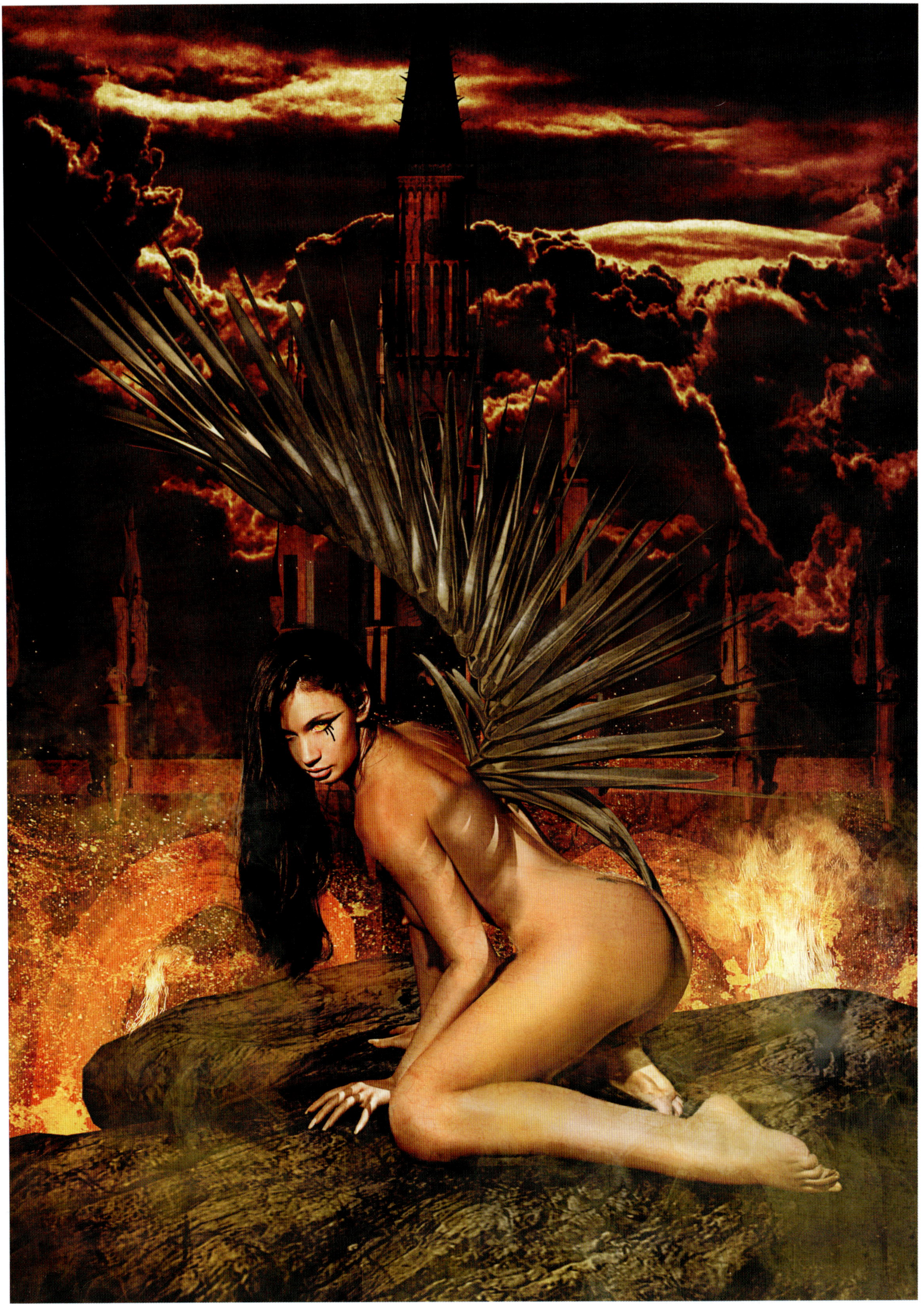

Hellbound

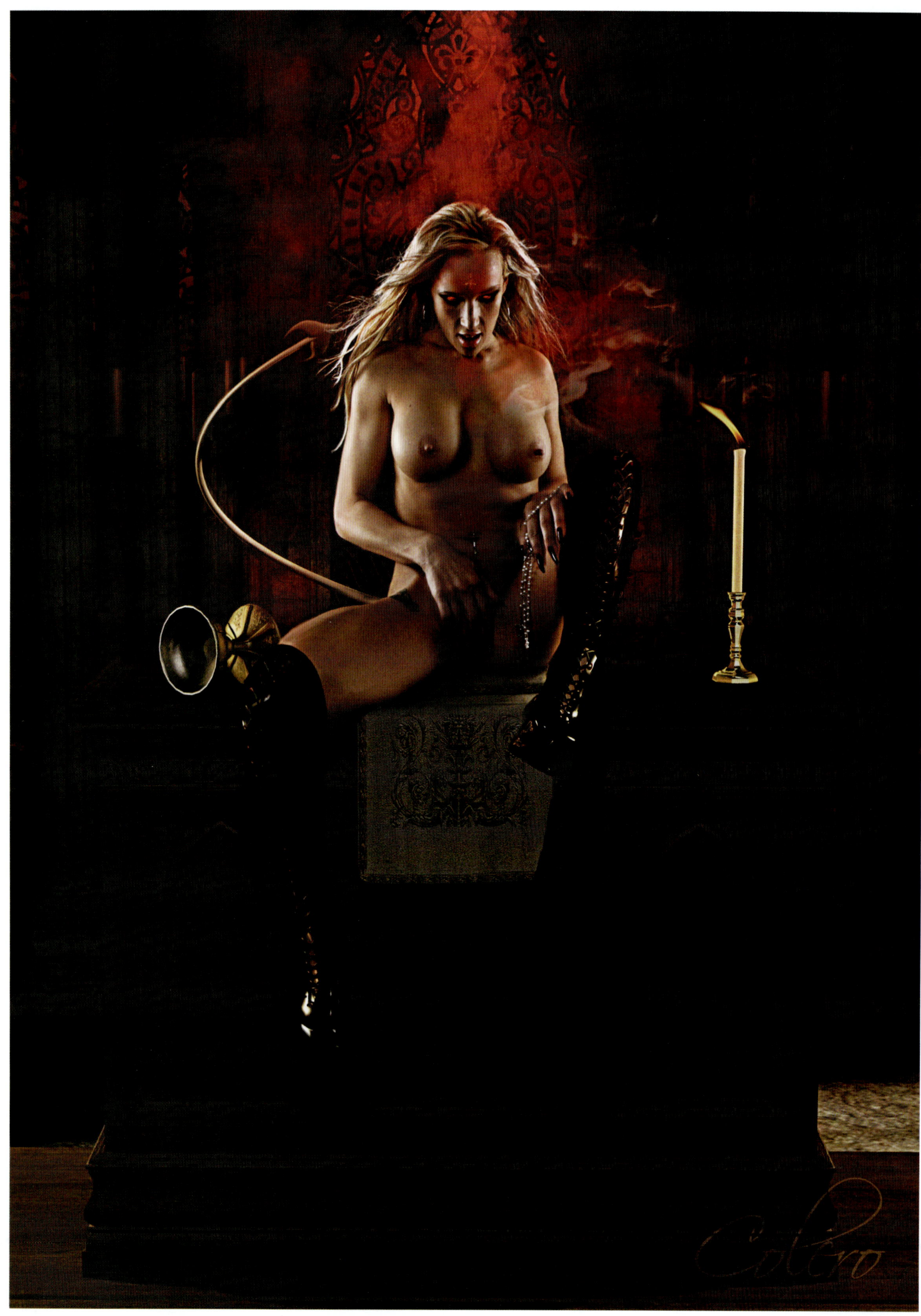

Blasphemy

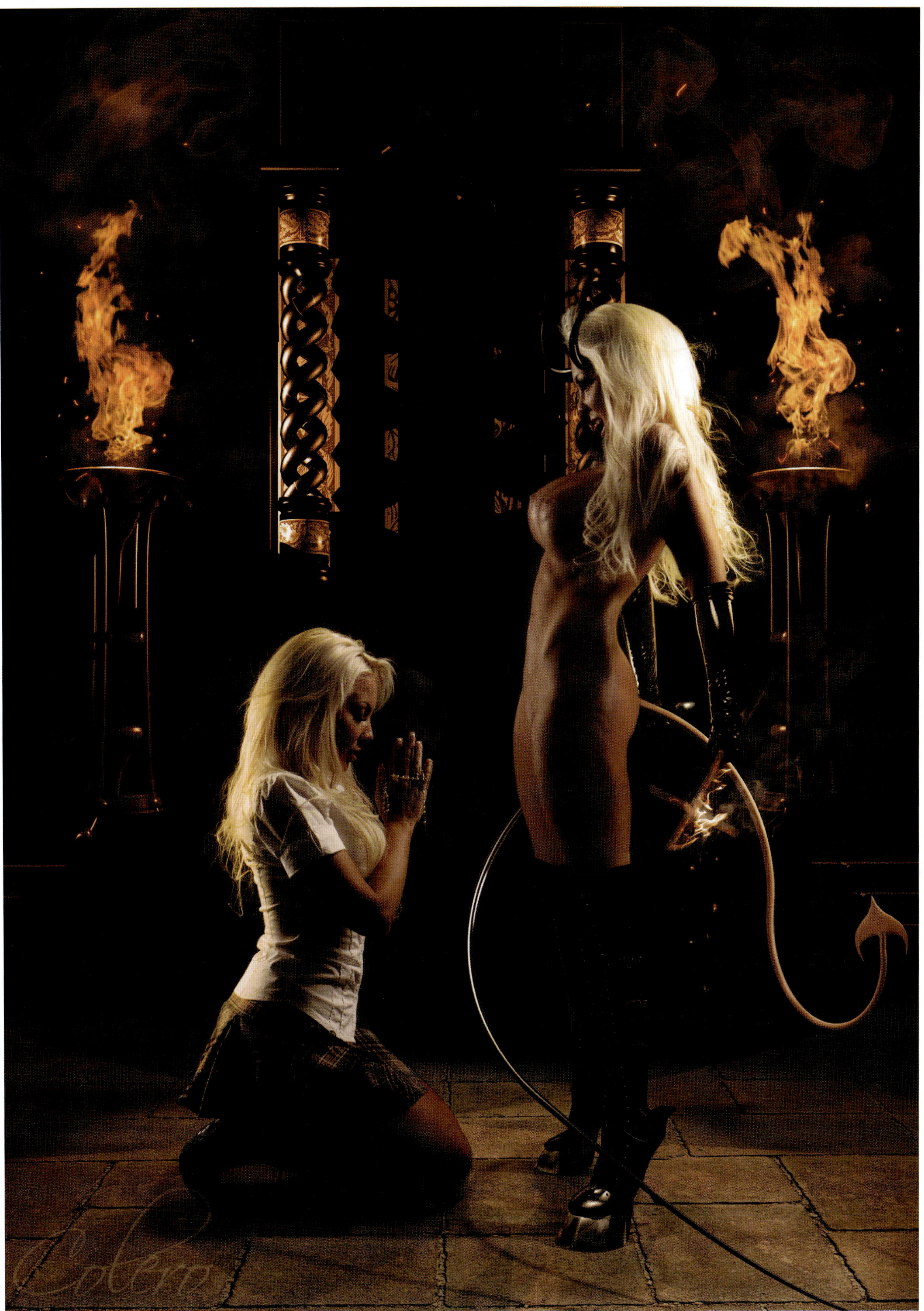

Midnight Confessions

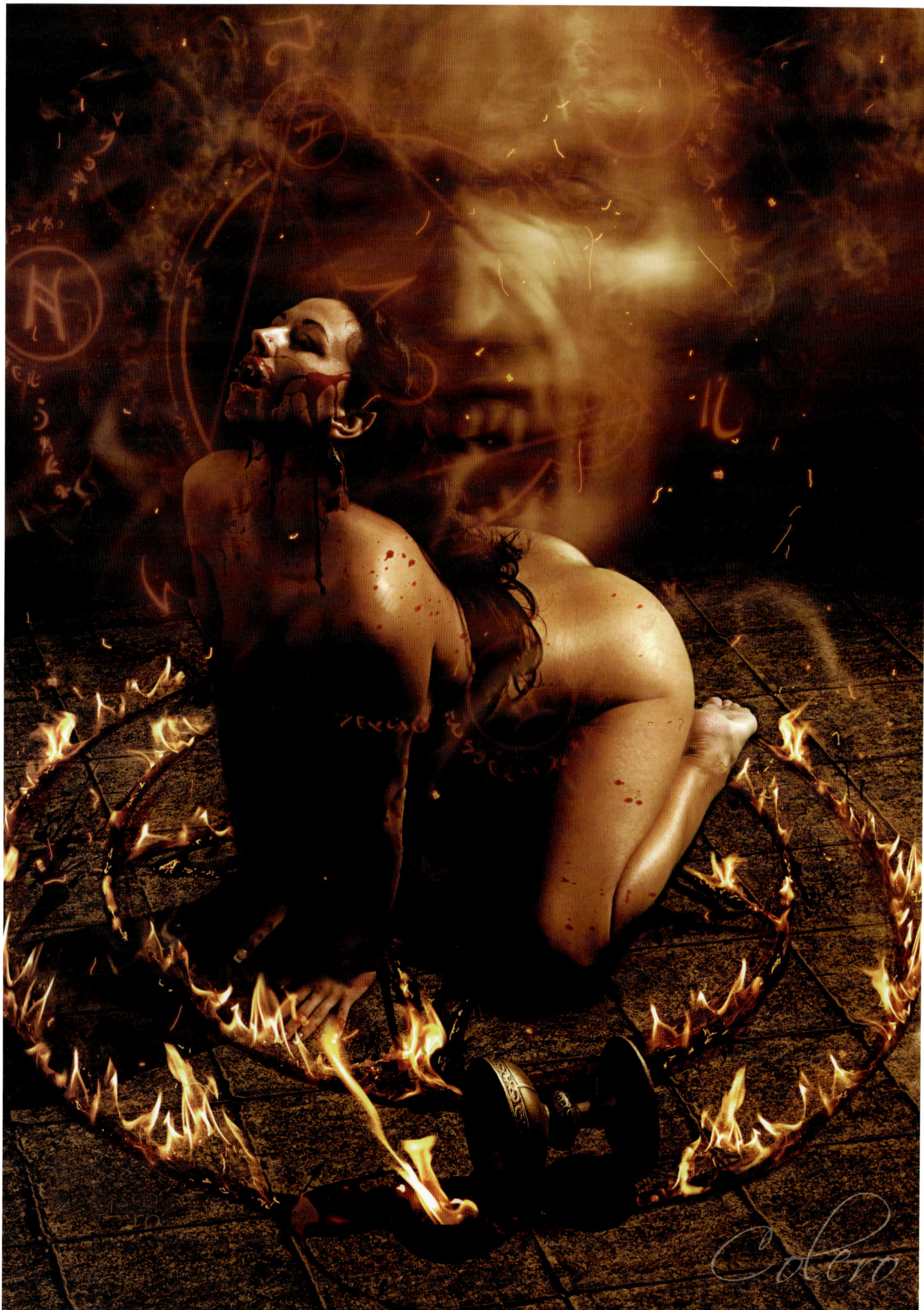

My Soul to Take

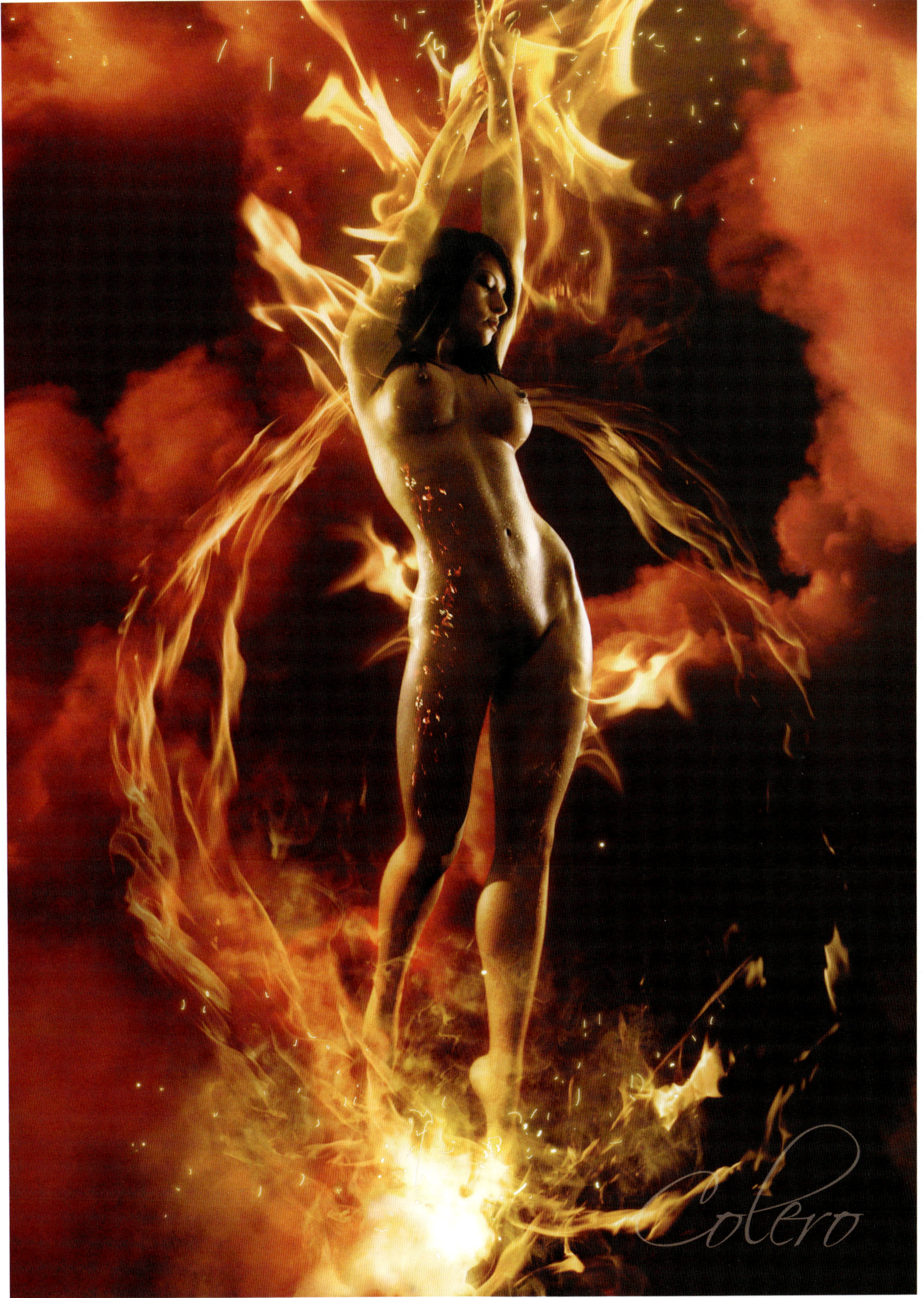

Phoenix

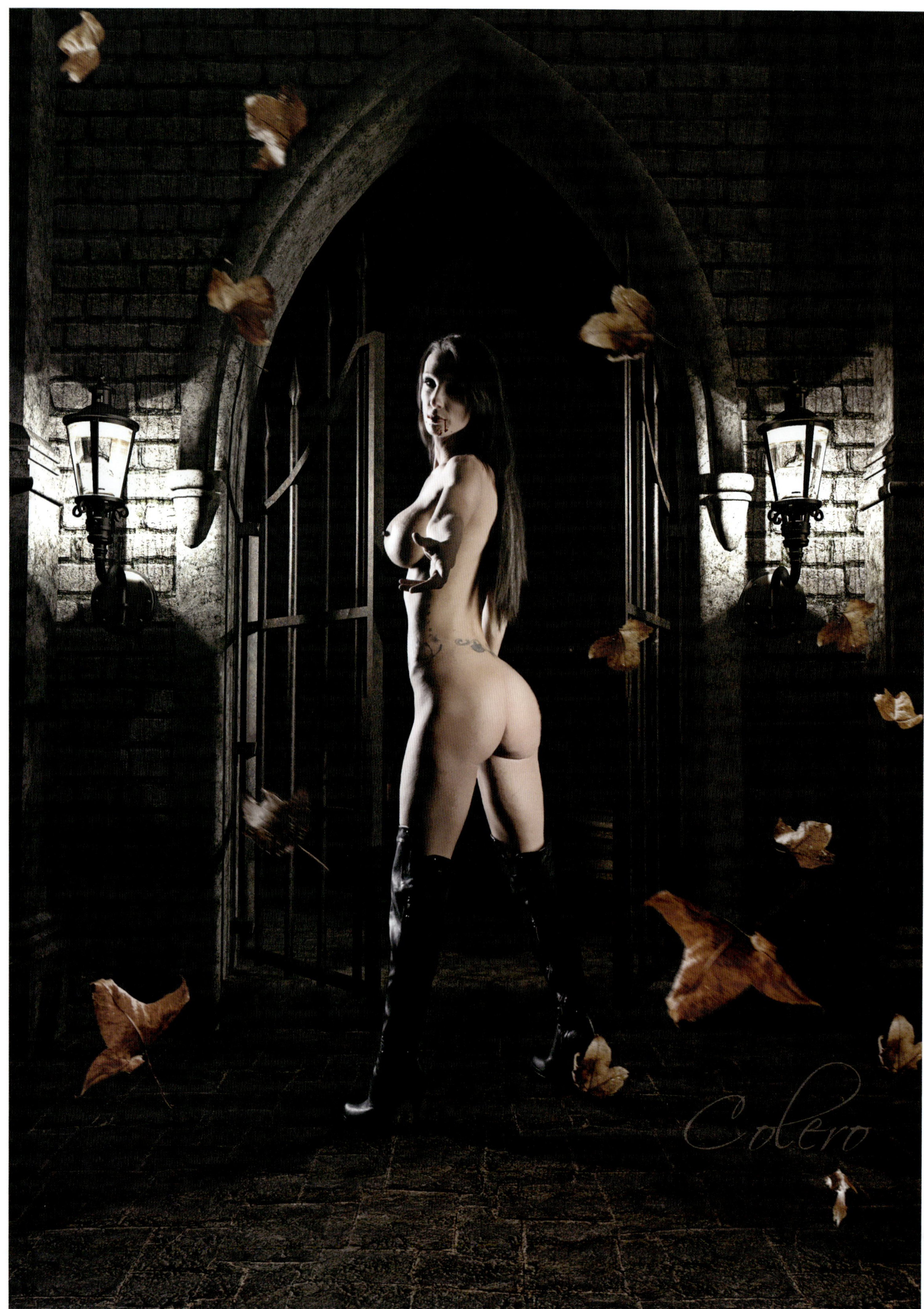

The Holy Dark

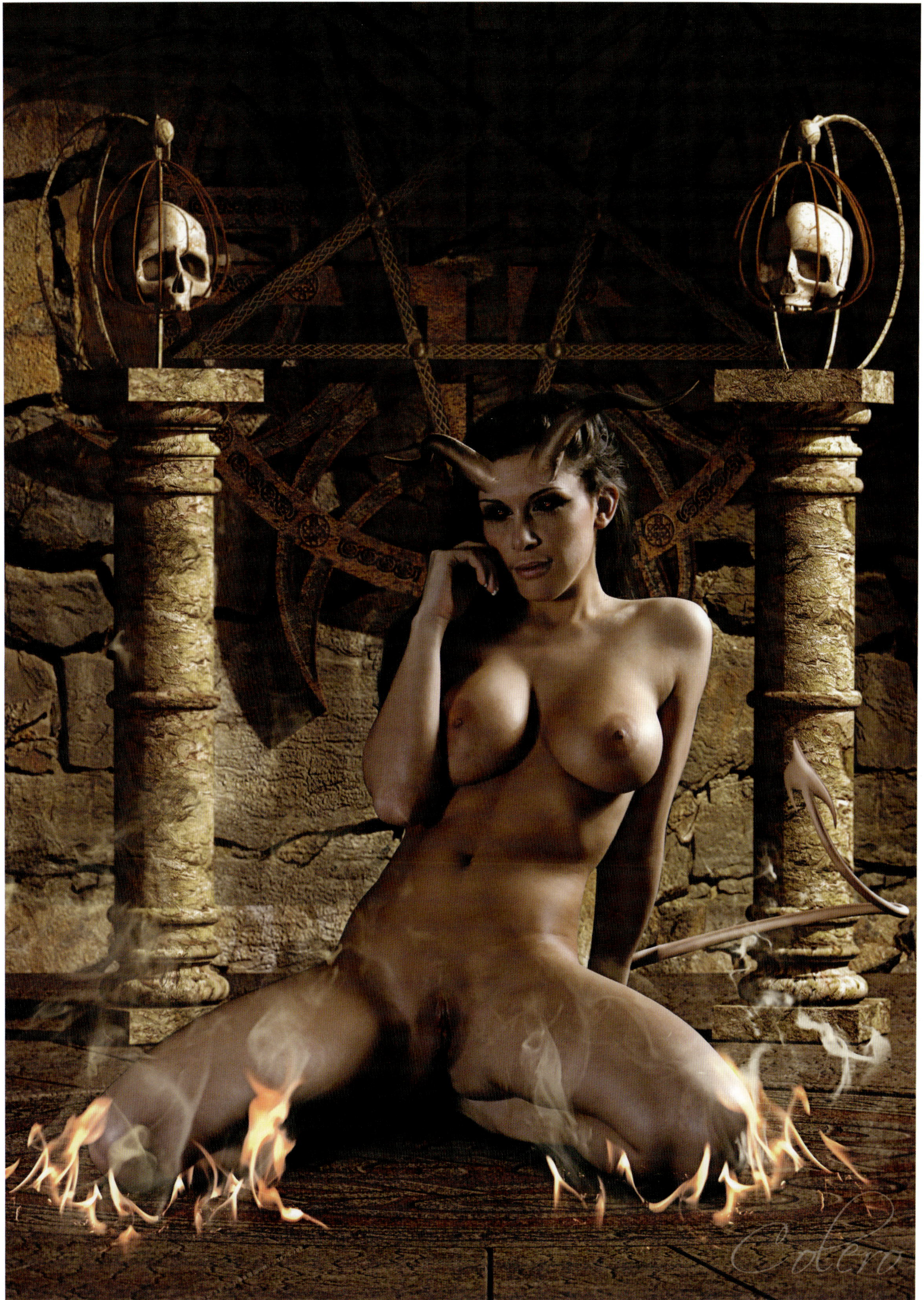

Temptation

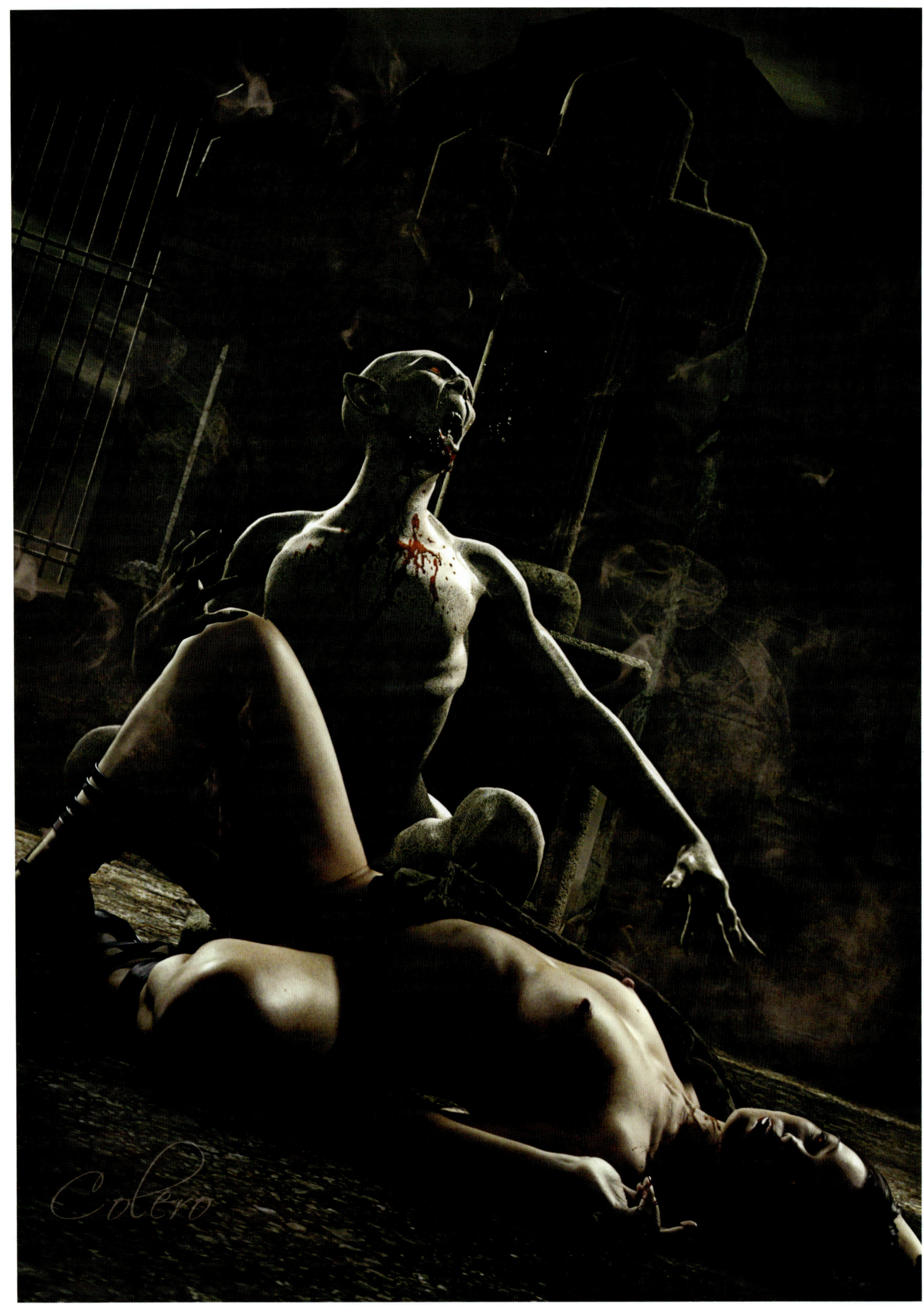

To All Good Things an End

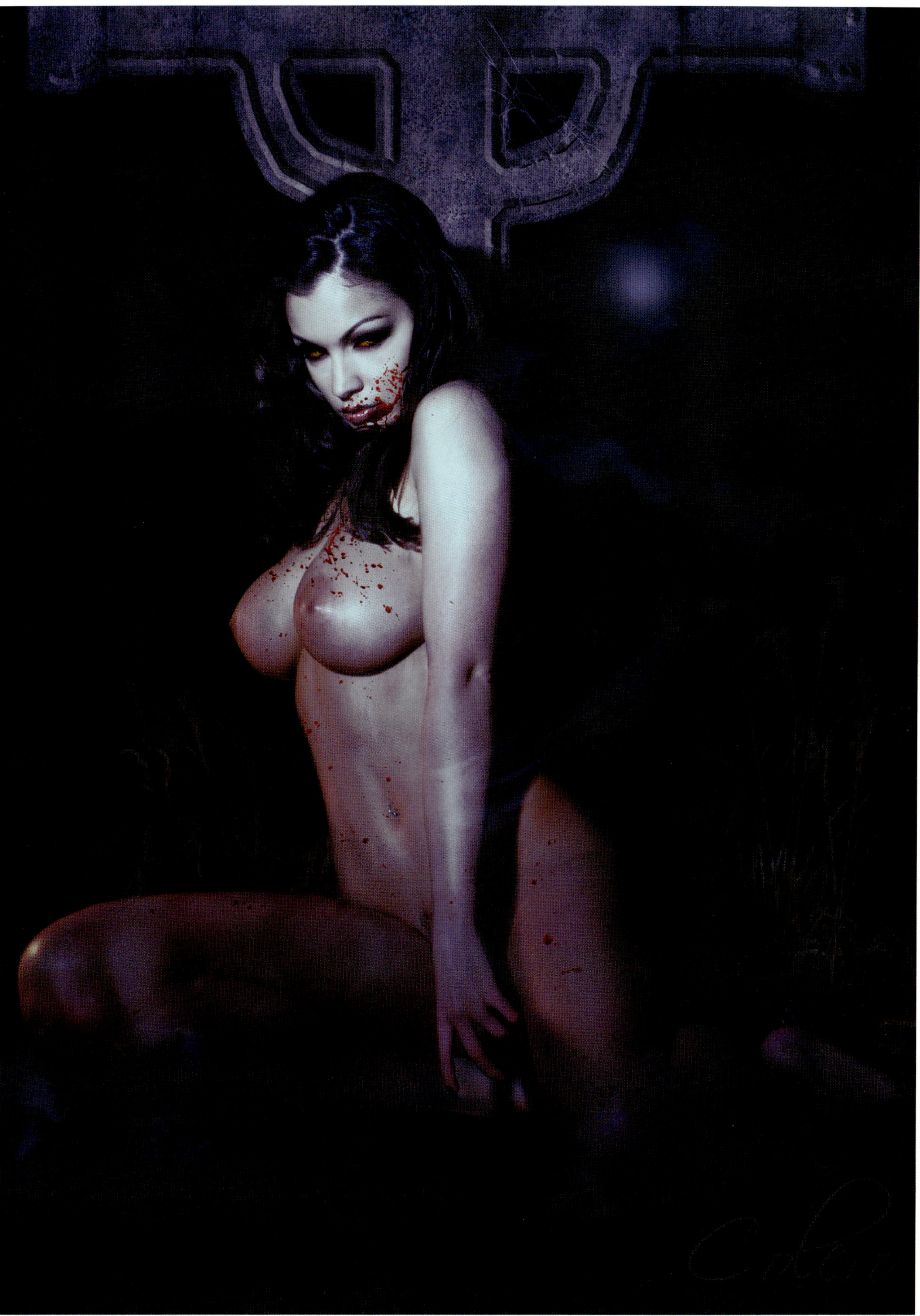

Invite Darkness

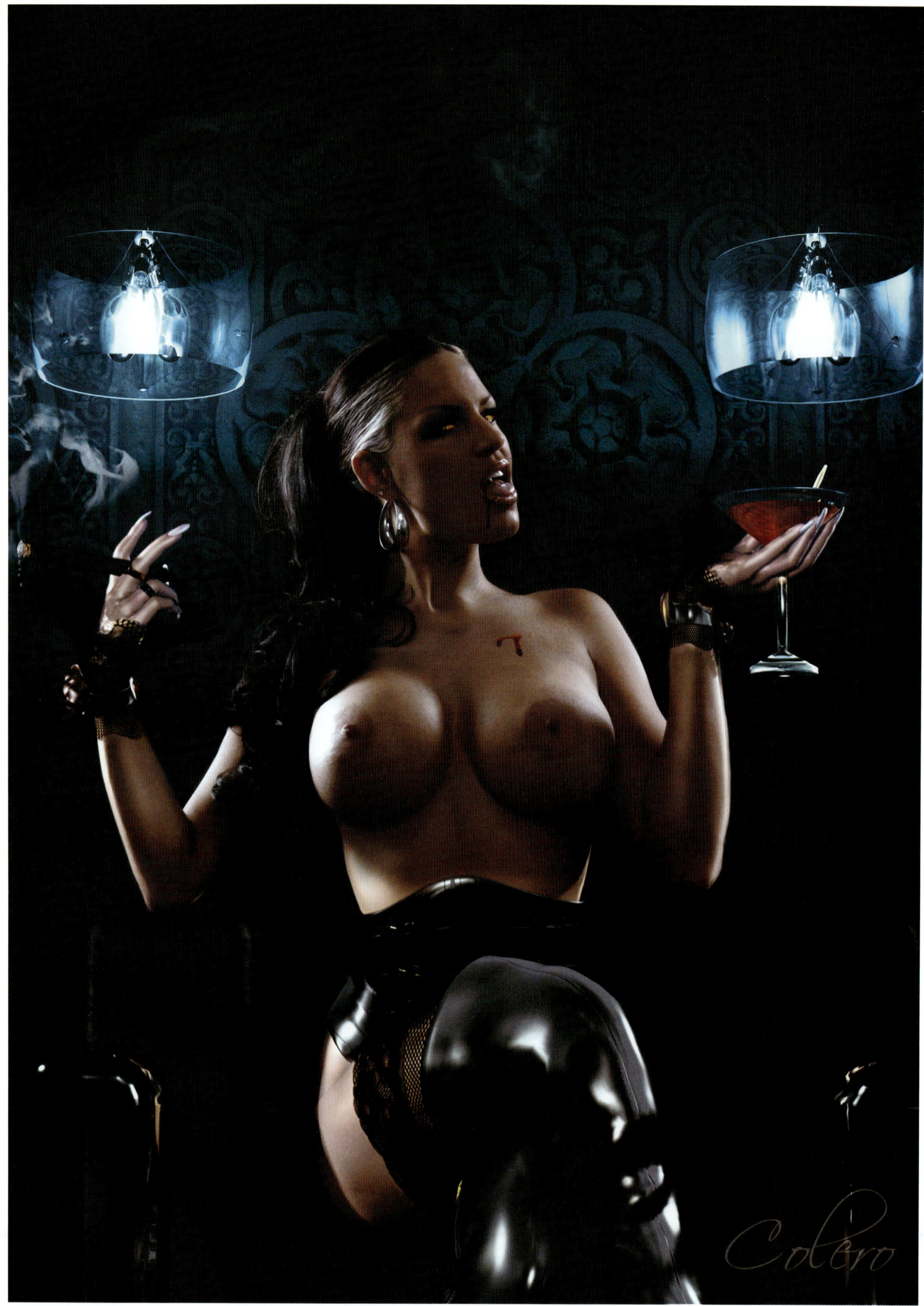

Lilith

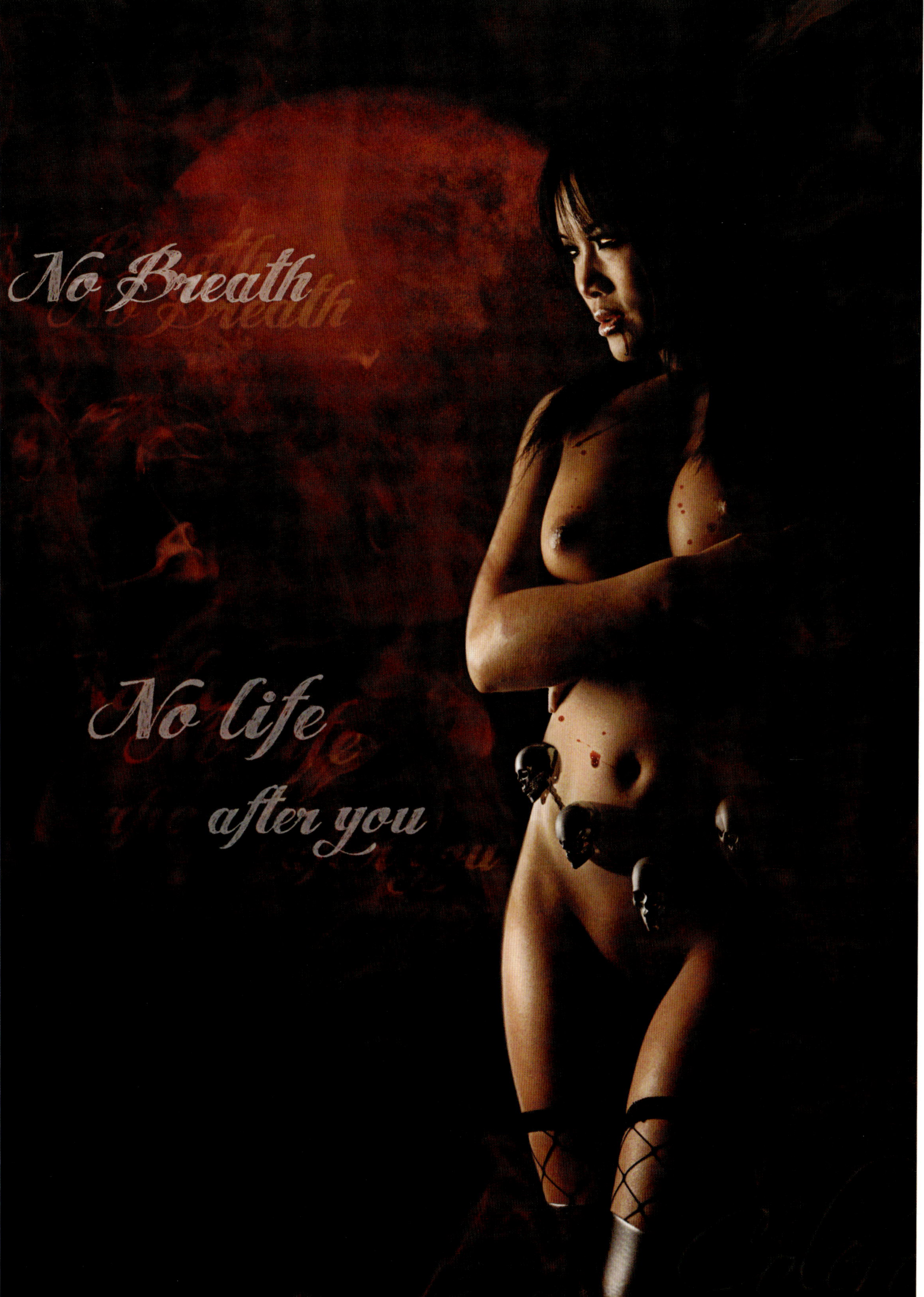

New Moon

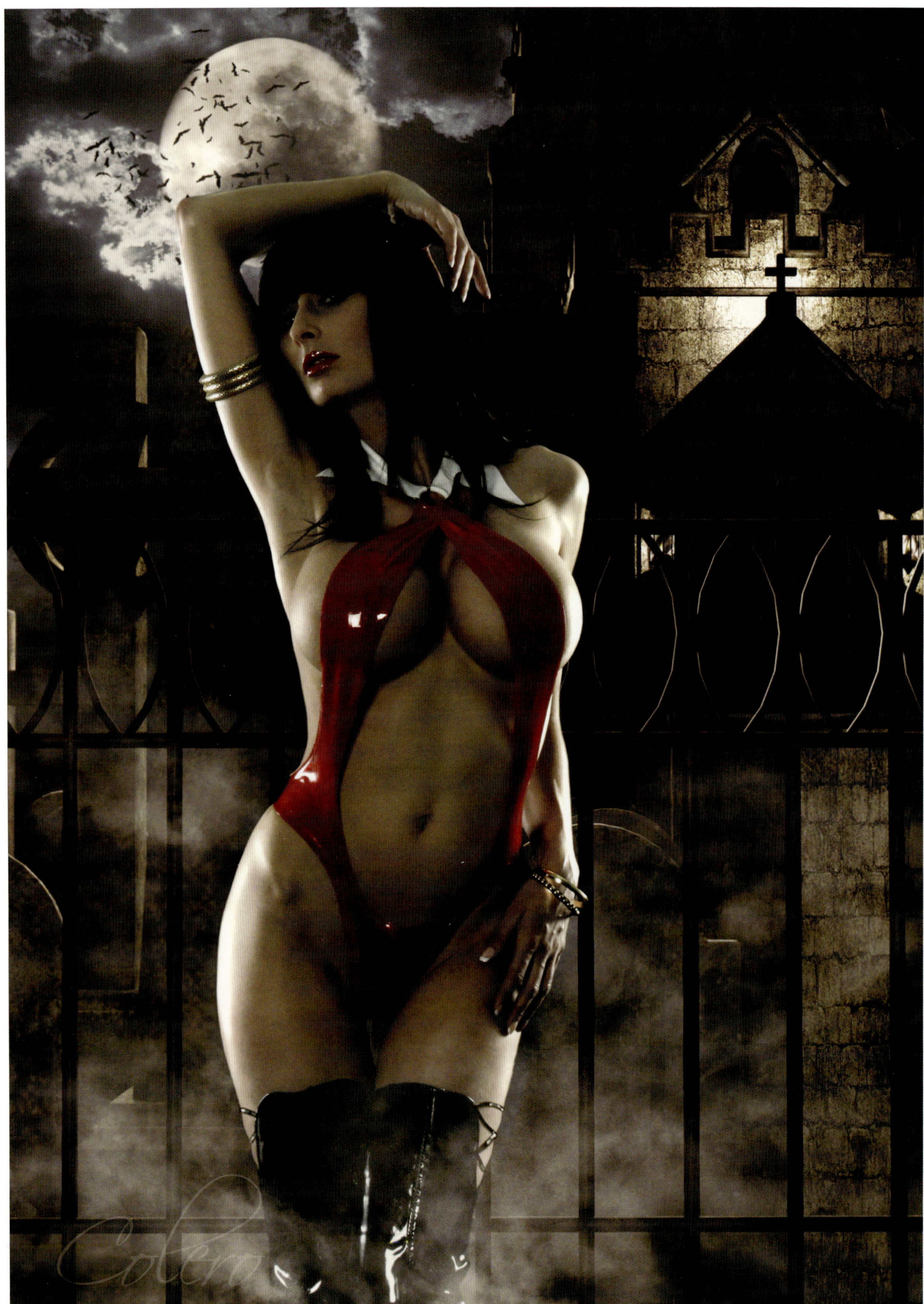

Fangtastic

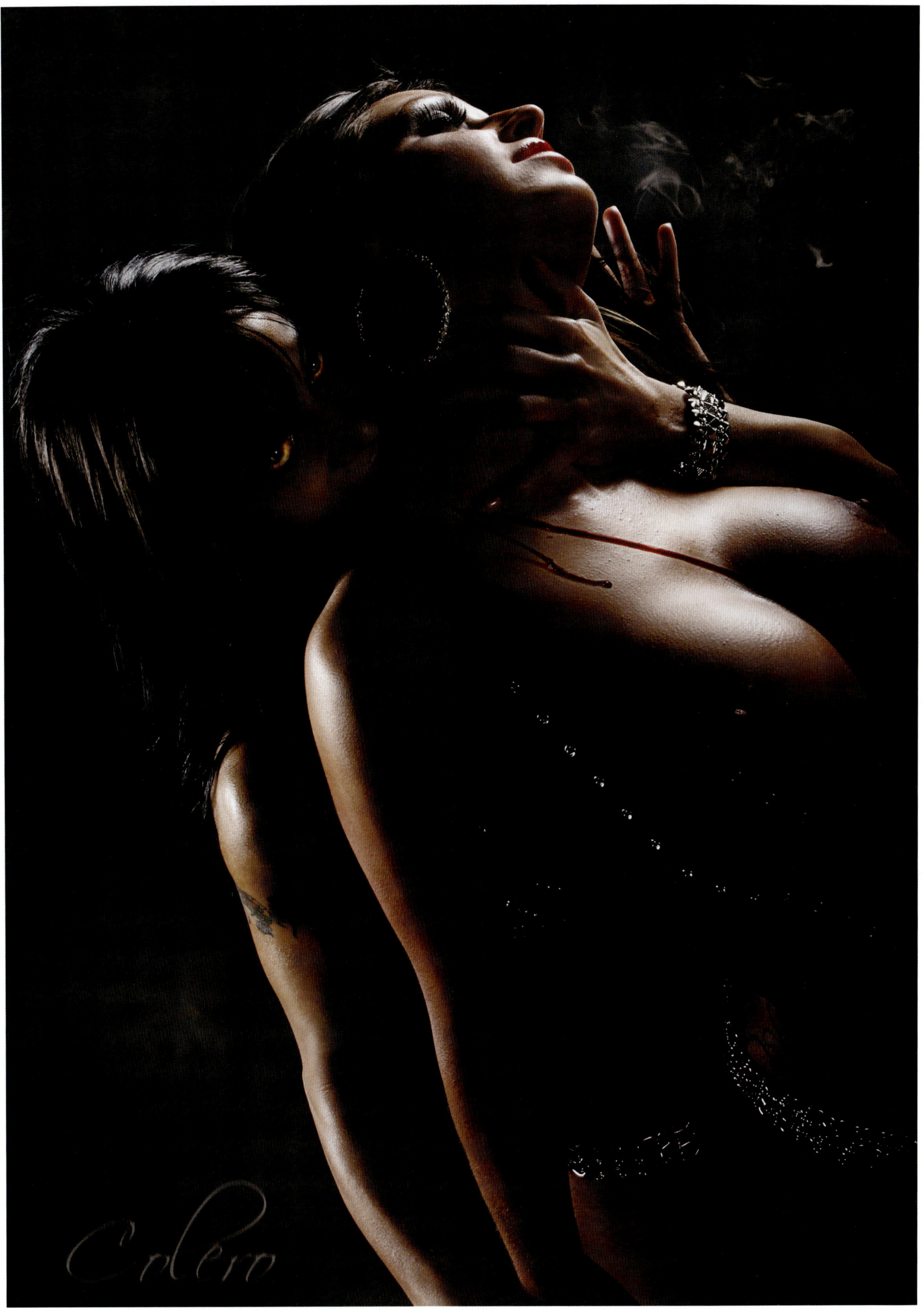

The Hunger

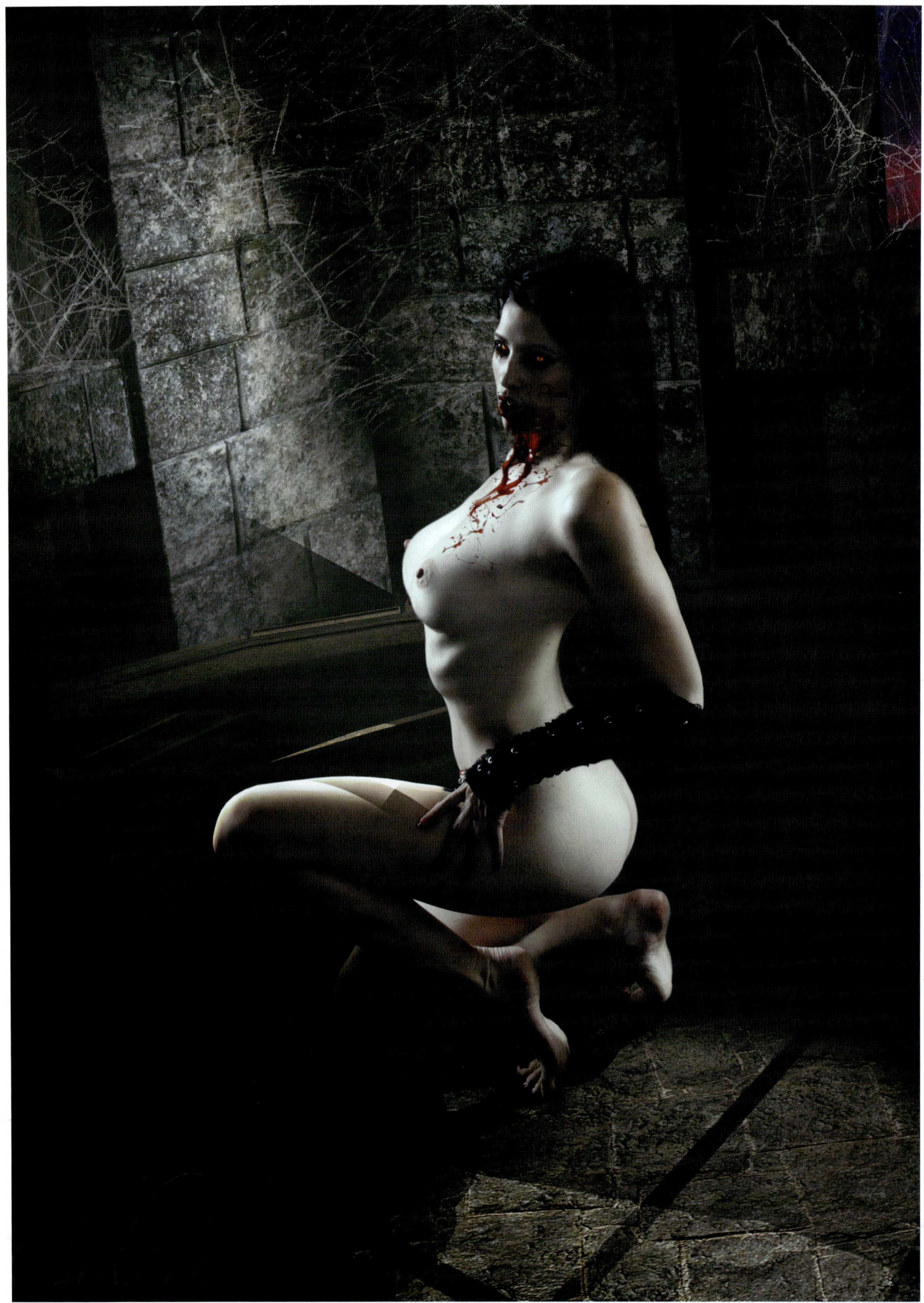

Tortured Soul

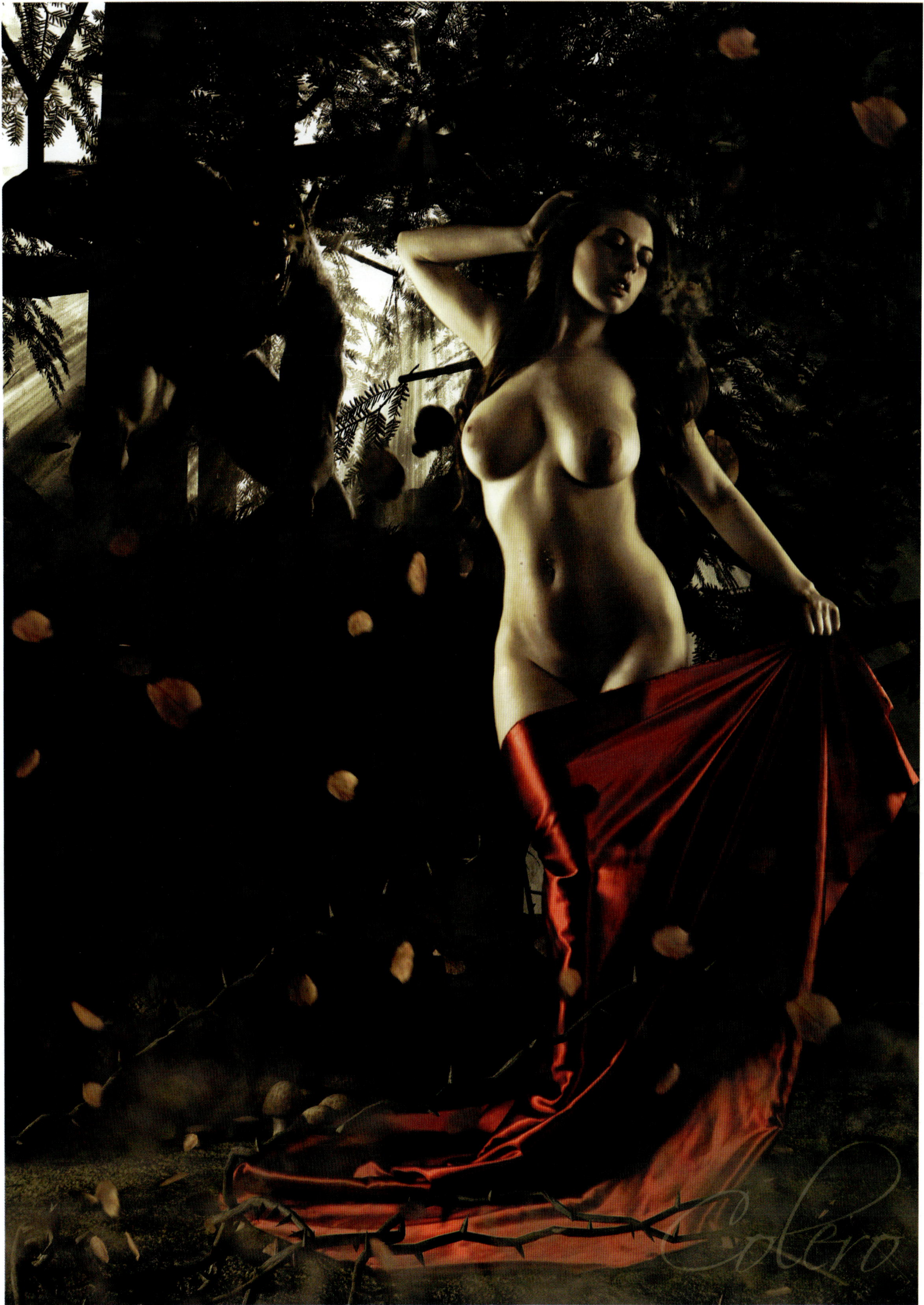

Cry Wolf

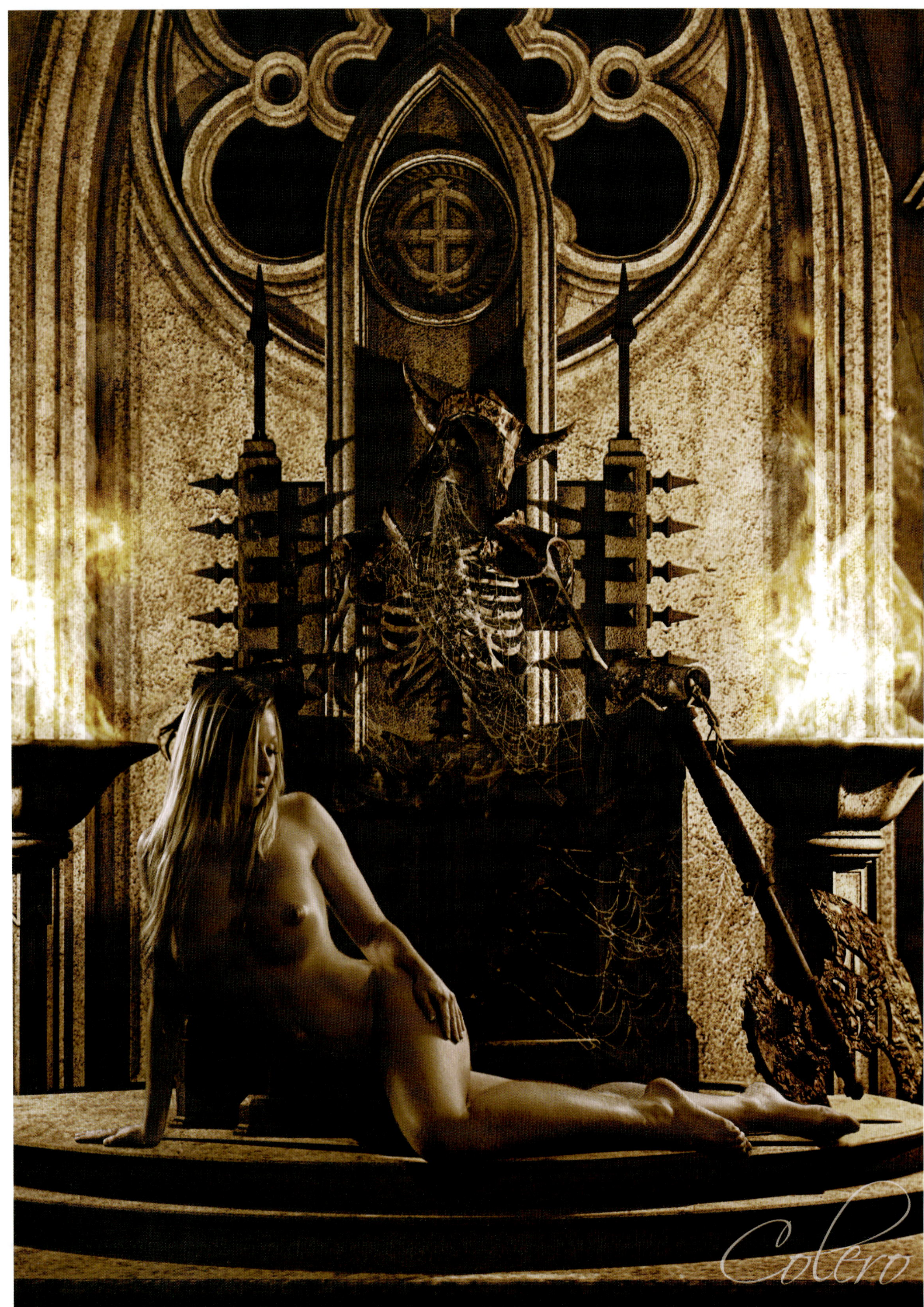

The Love You Save

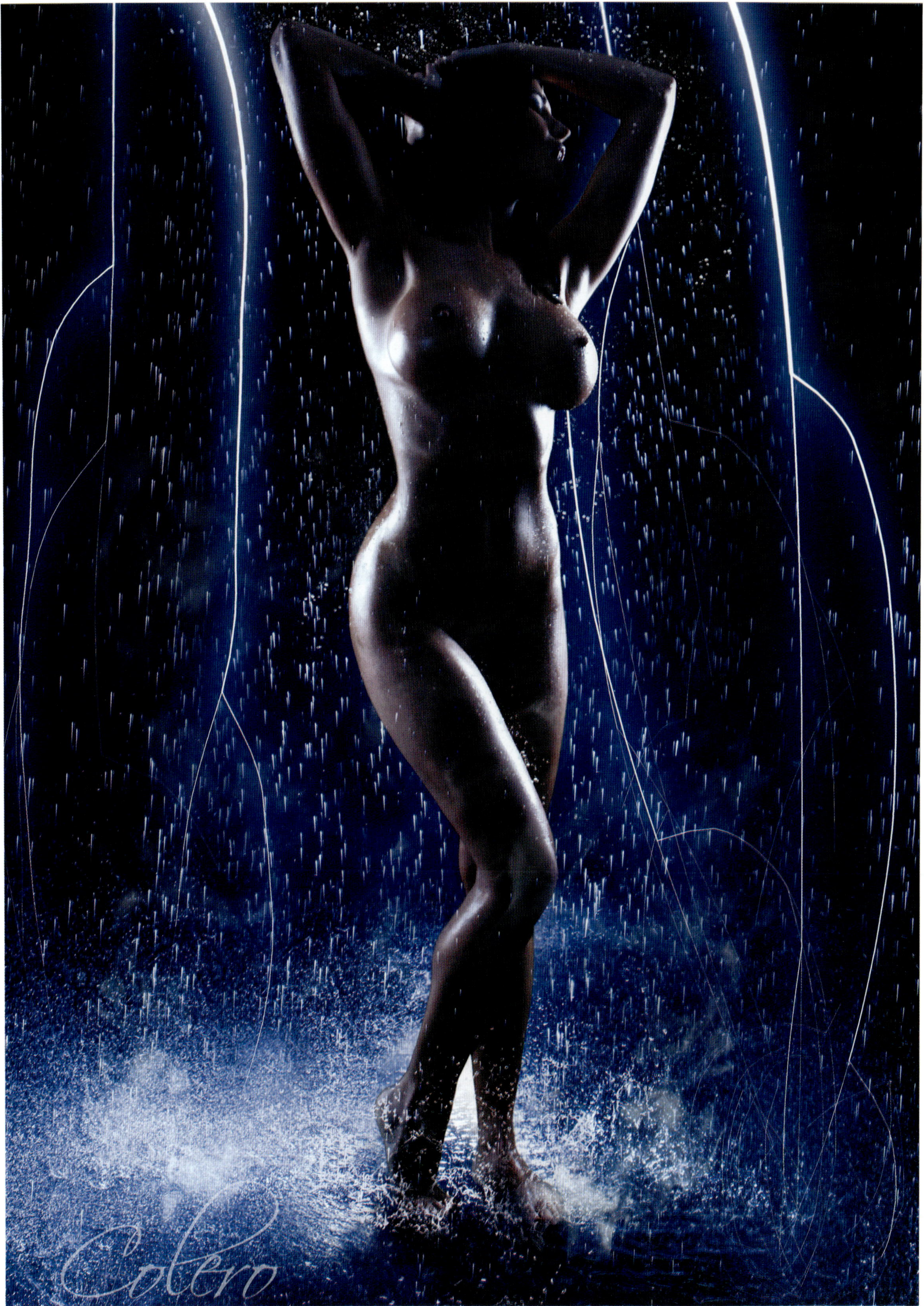

Storm

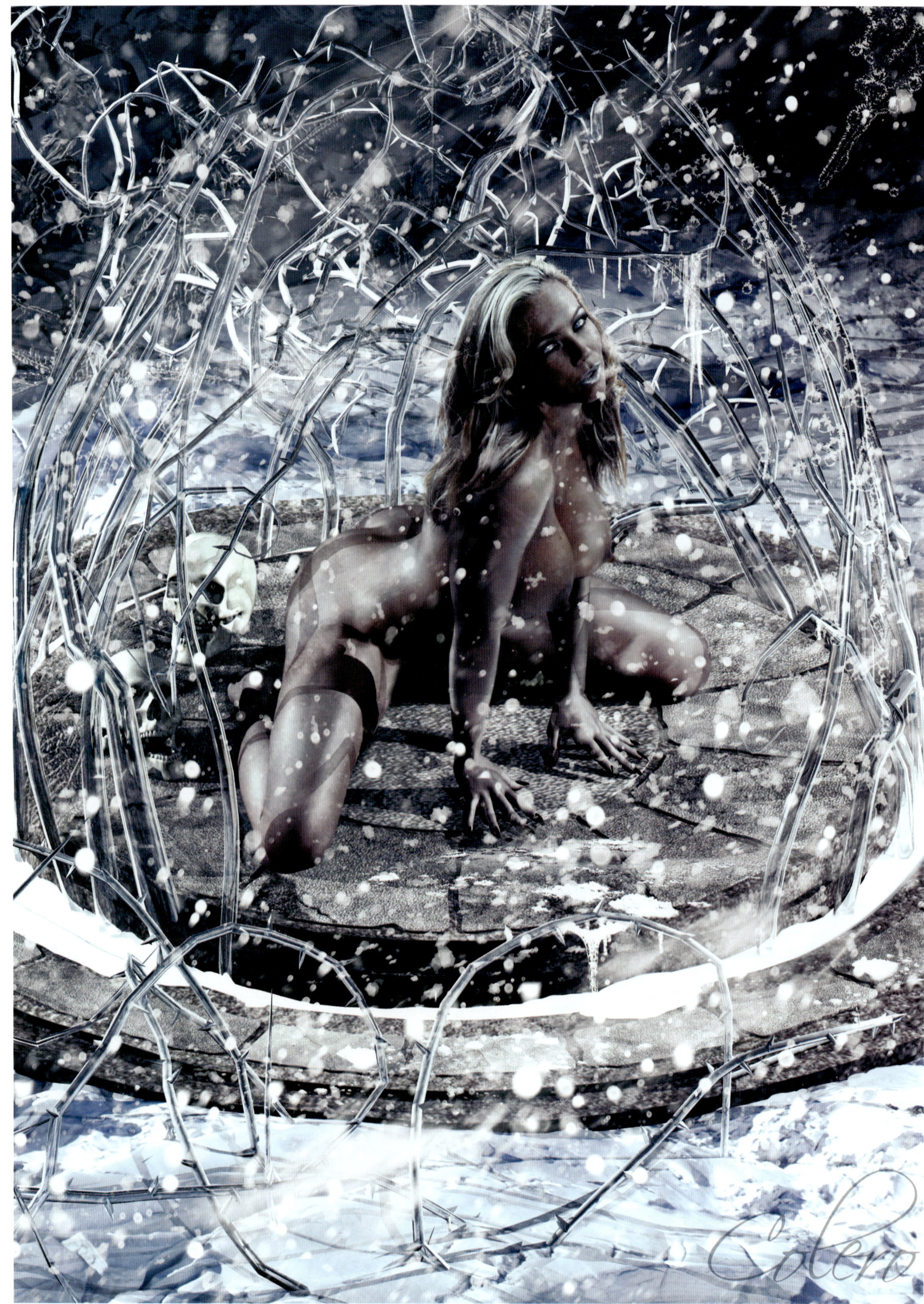

And Your Soul of Ice

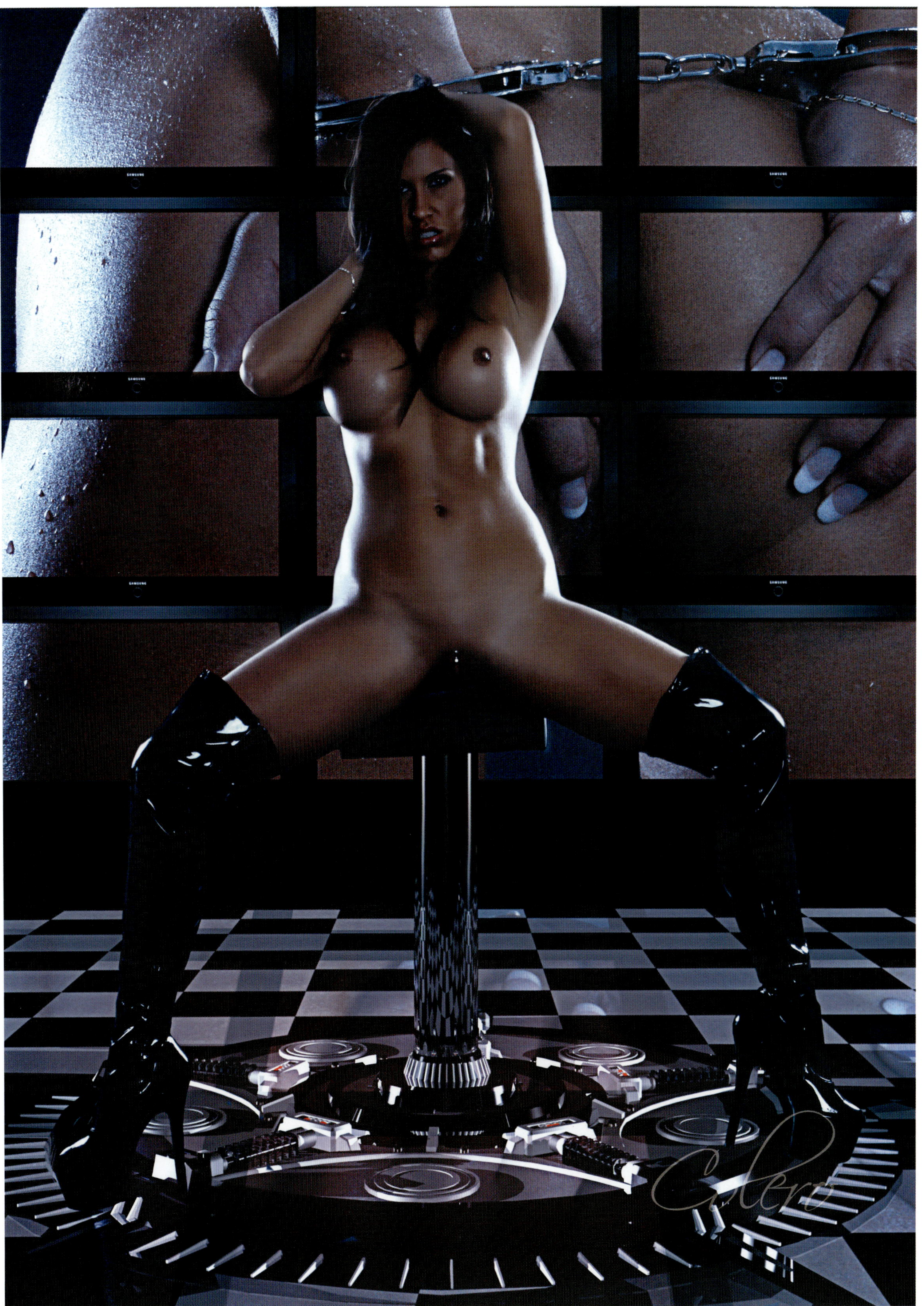

Video Vamp

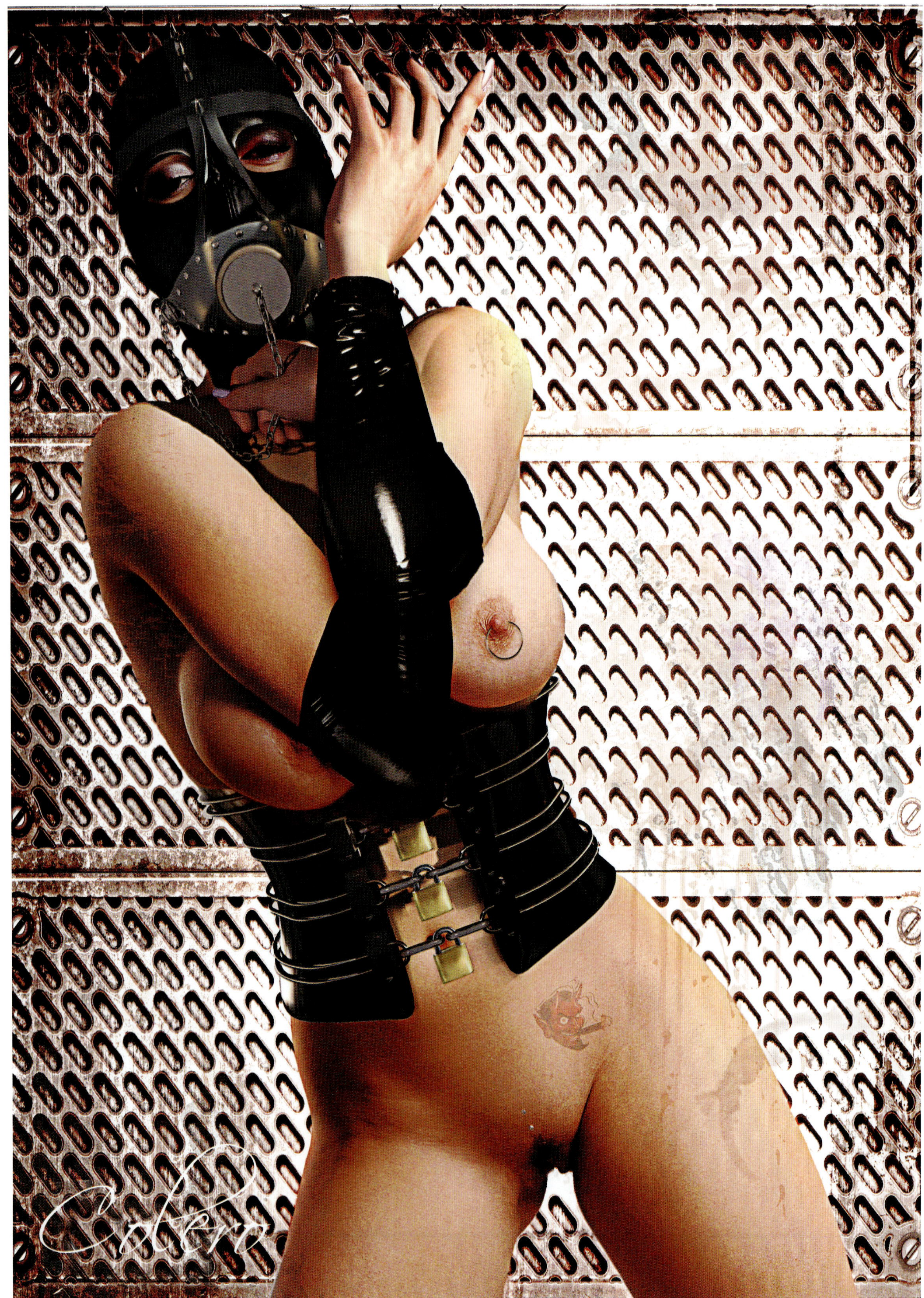

Twisted

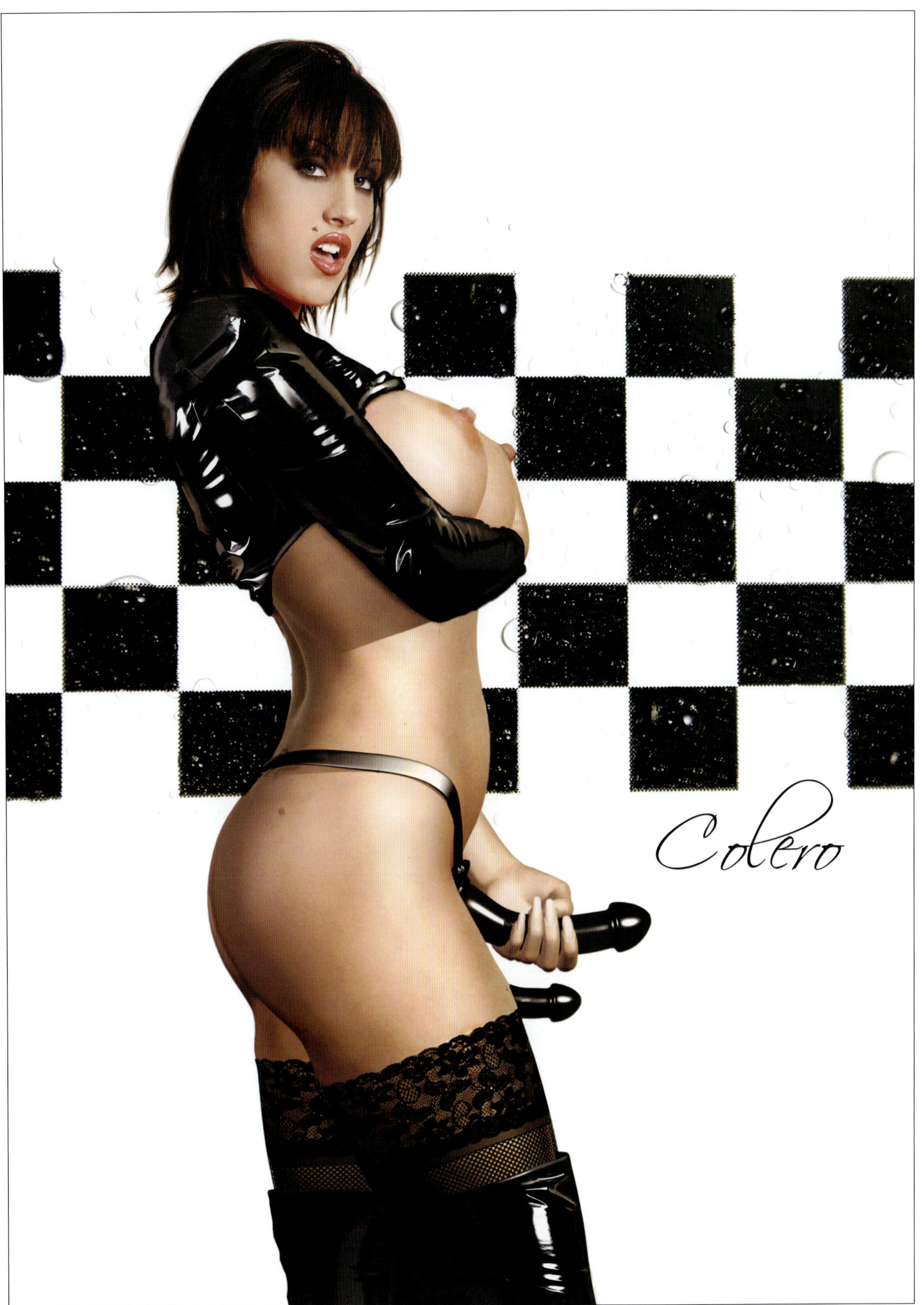
Colero

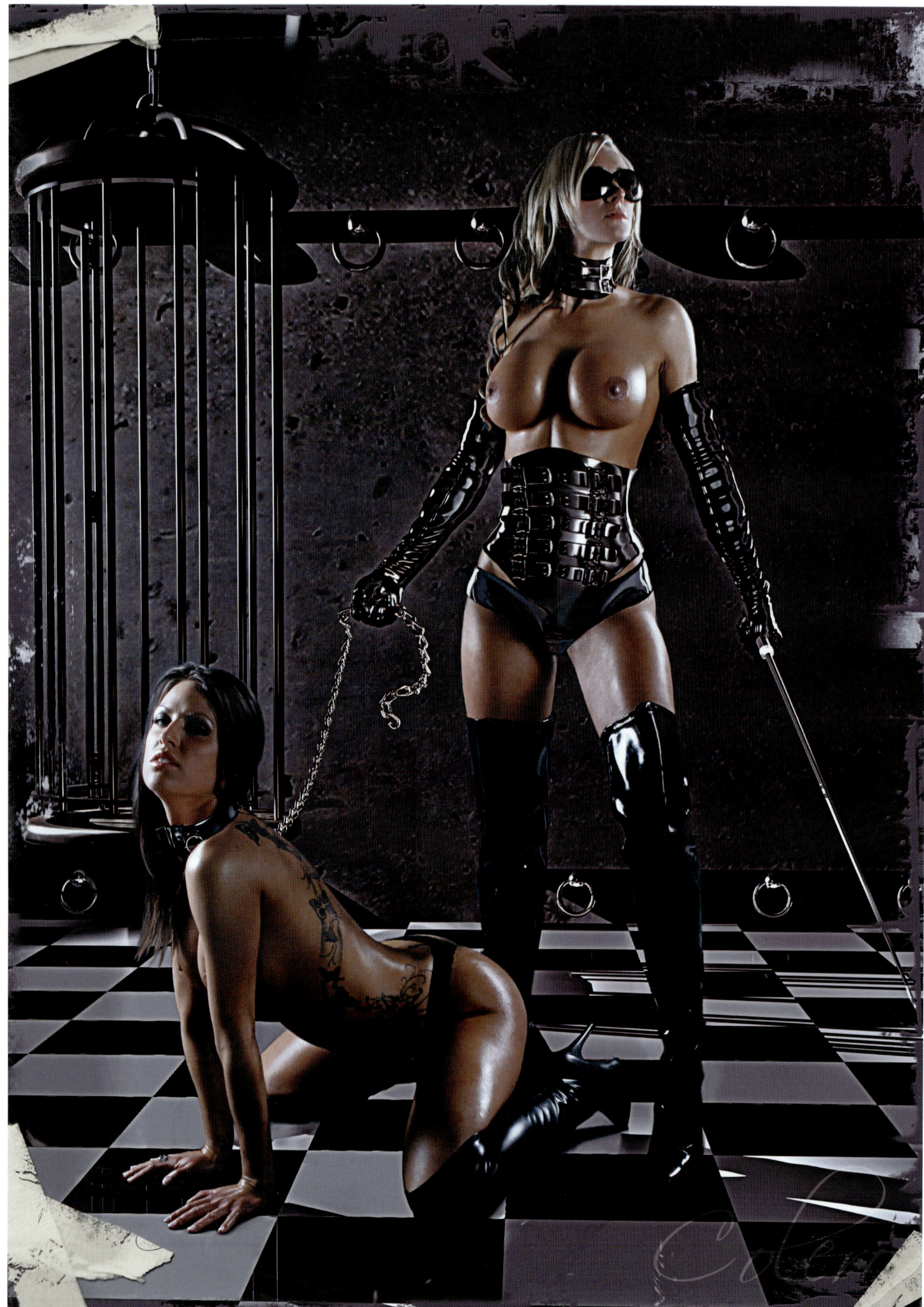

Upper Class

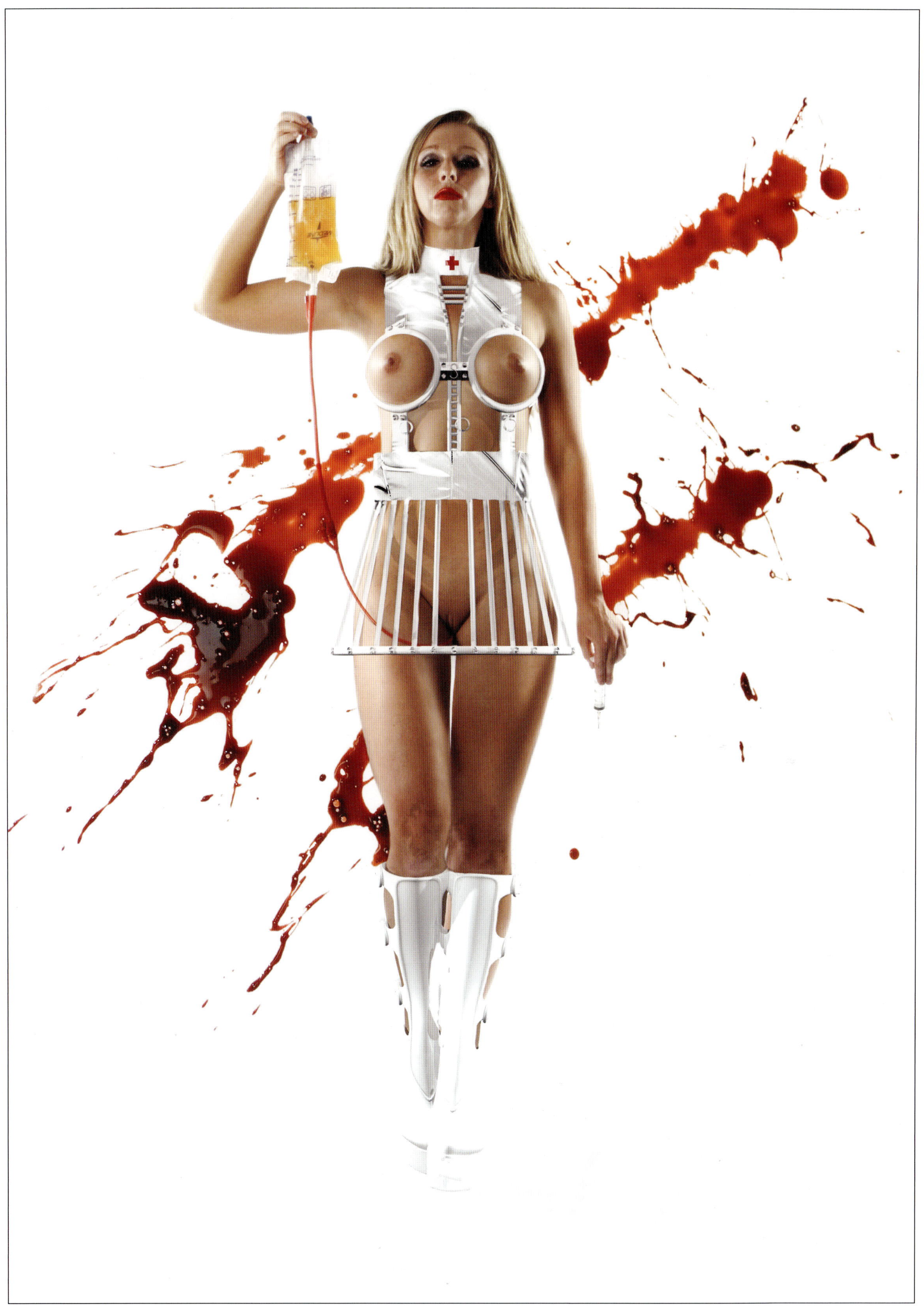

Nurse Ratchet

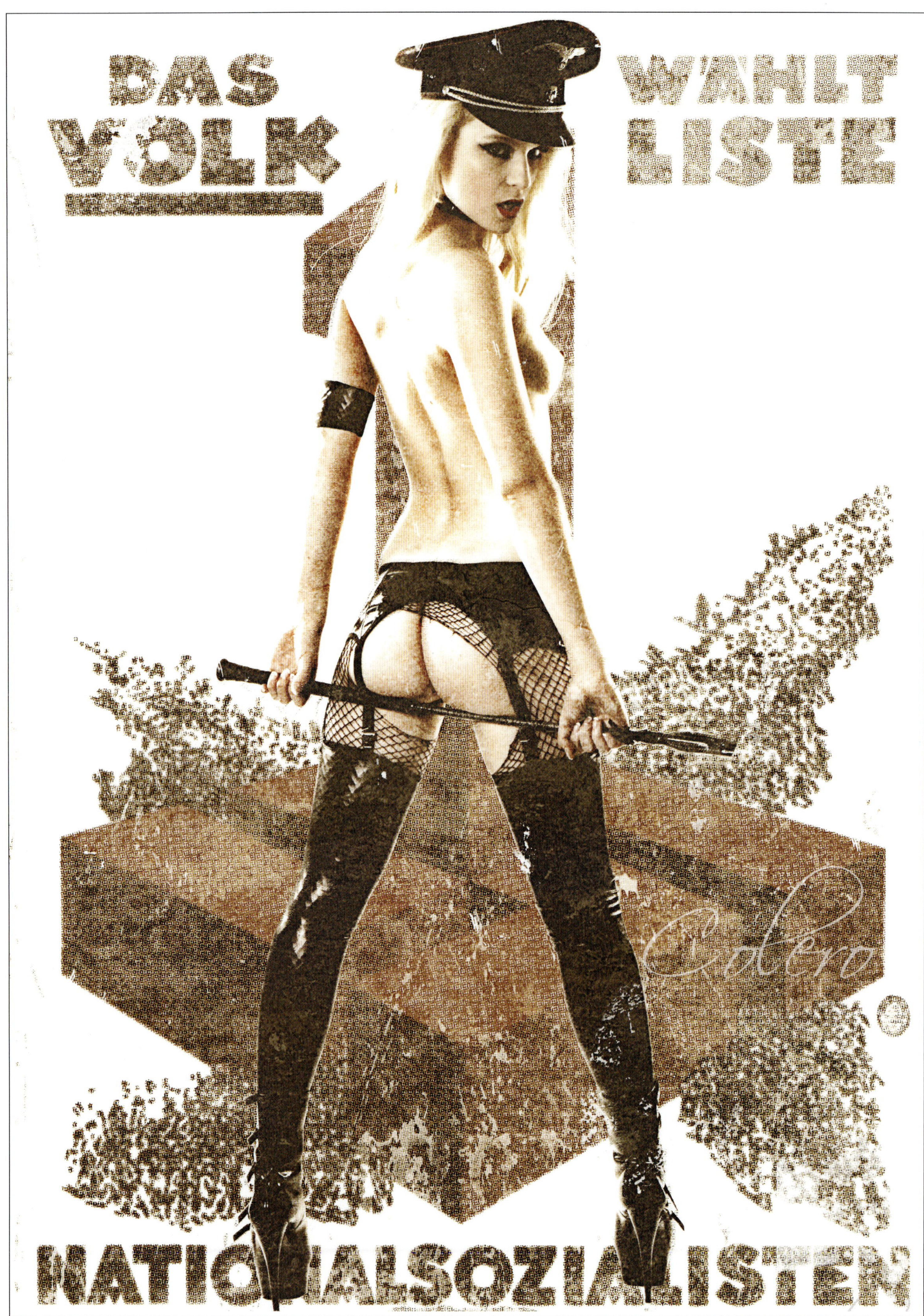

Achtung Baby

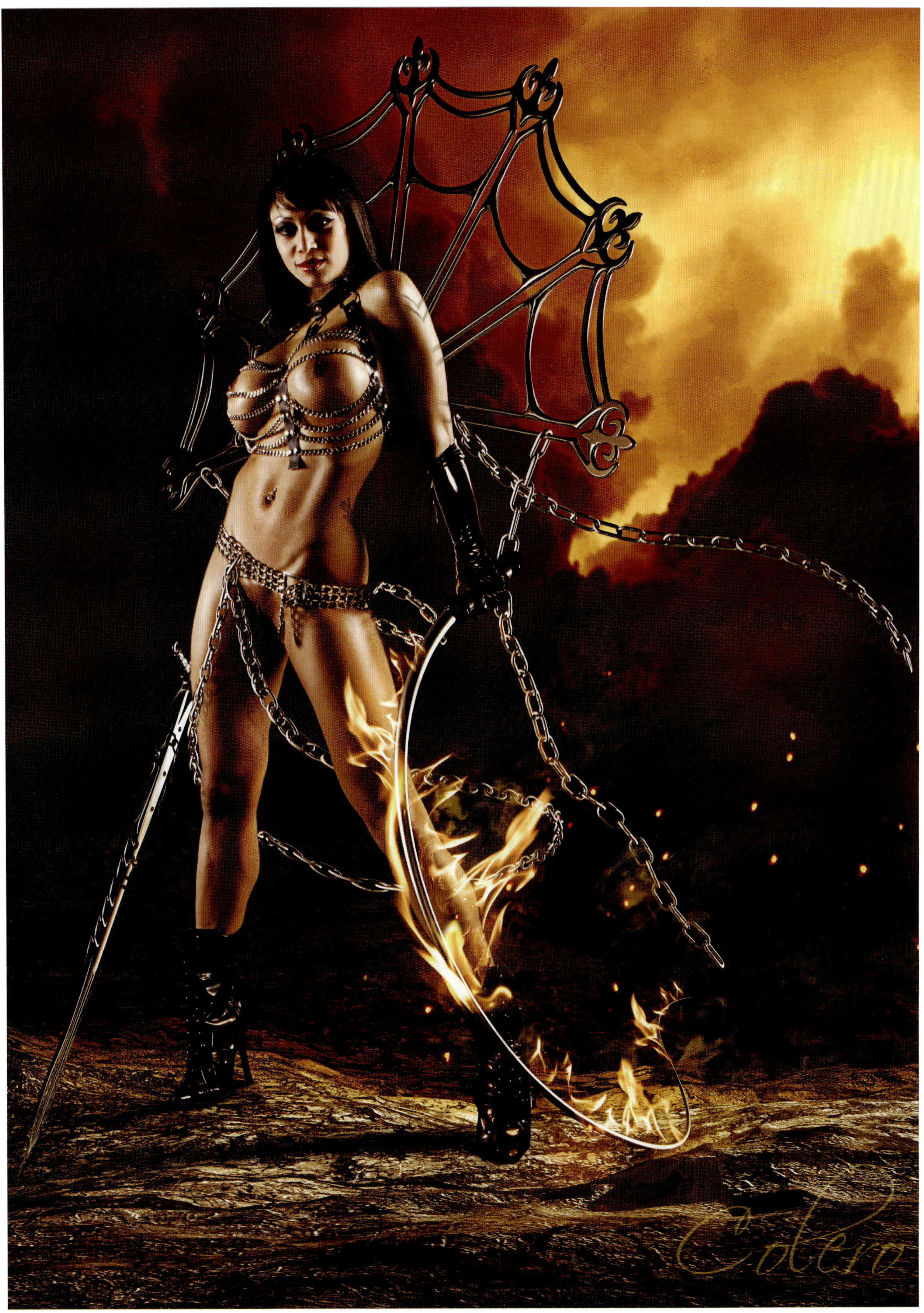

Dark Lady

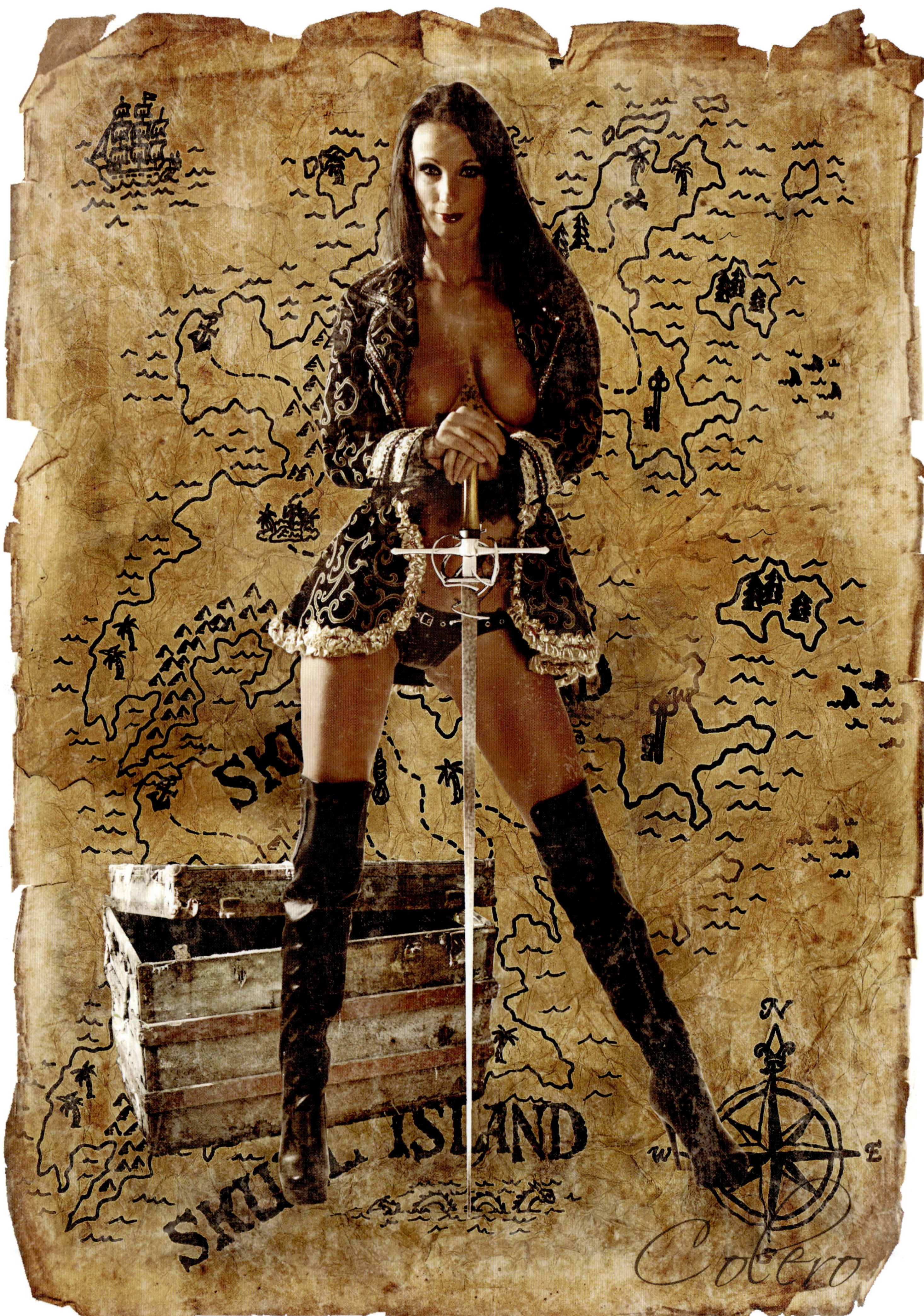

Rogue

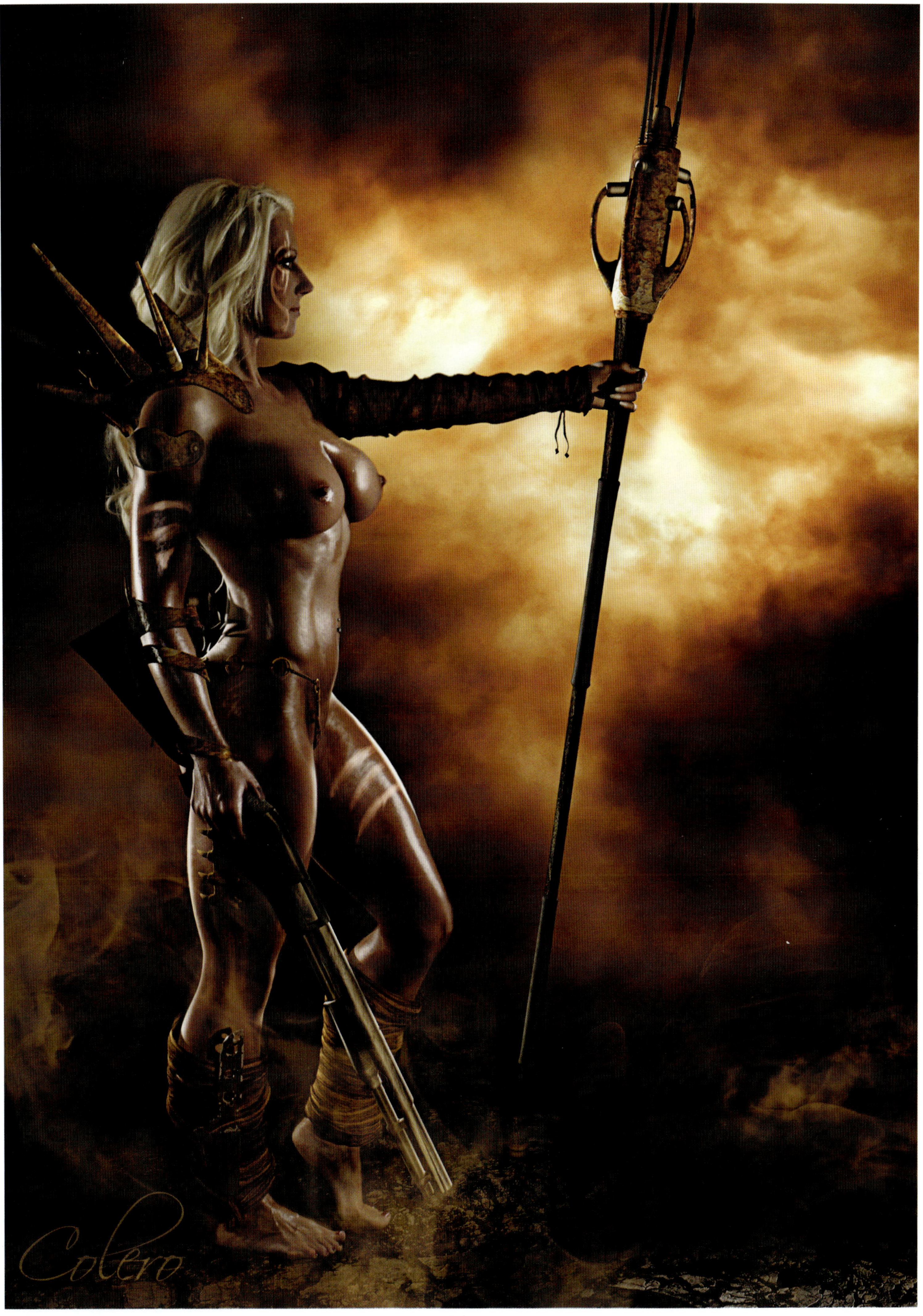

Ashes

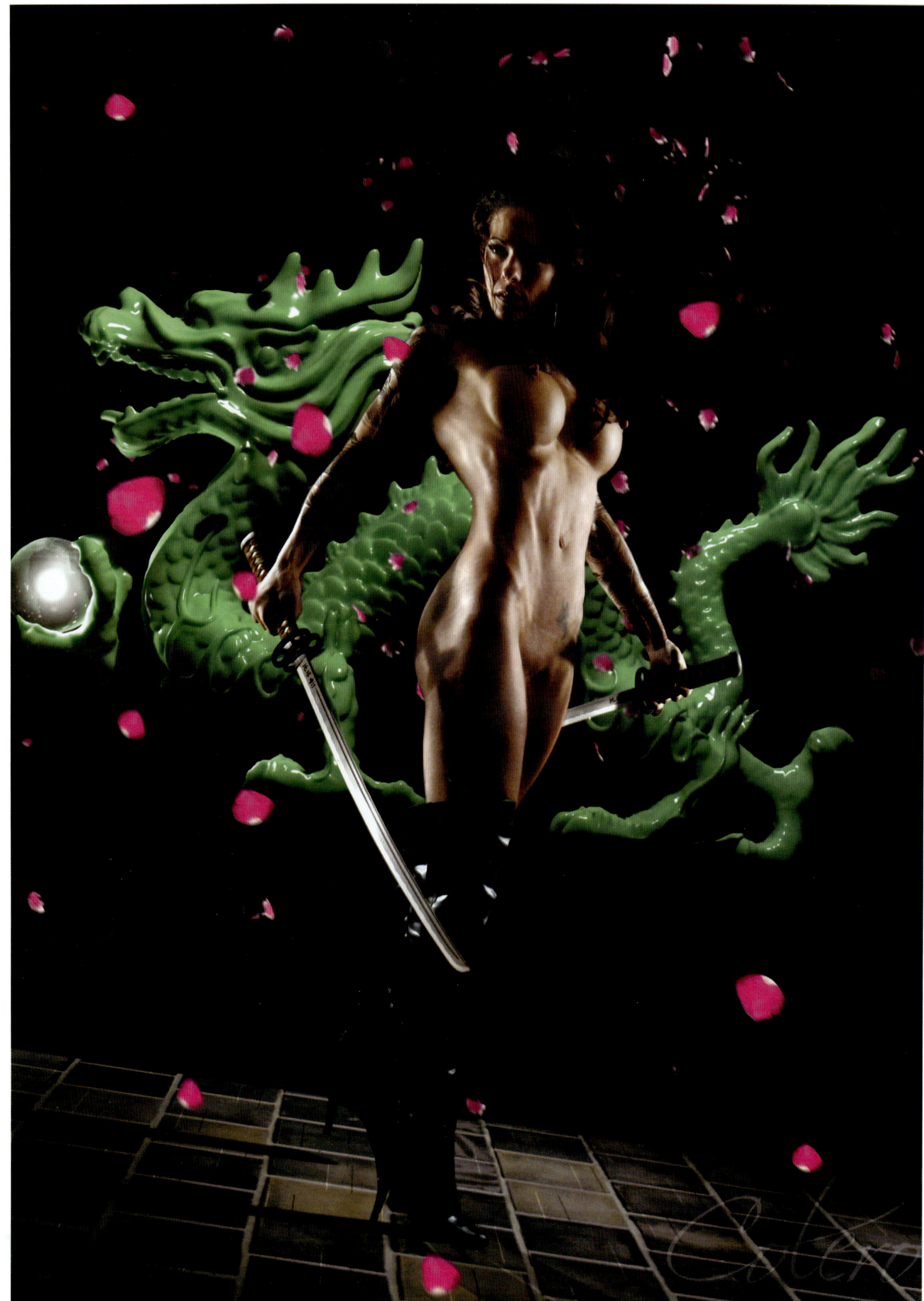

Jade Dragon

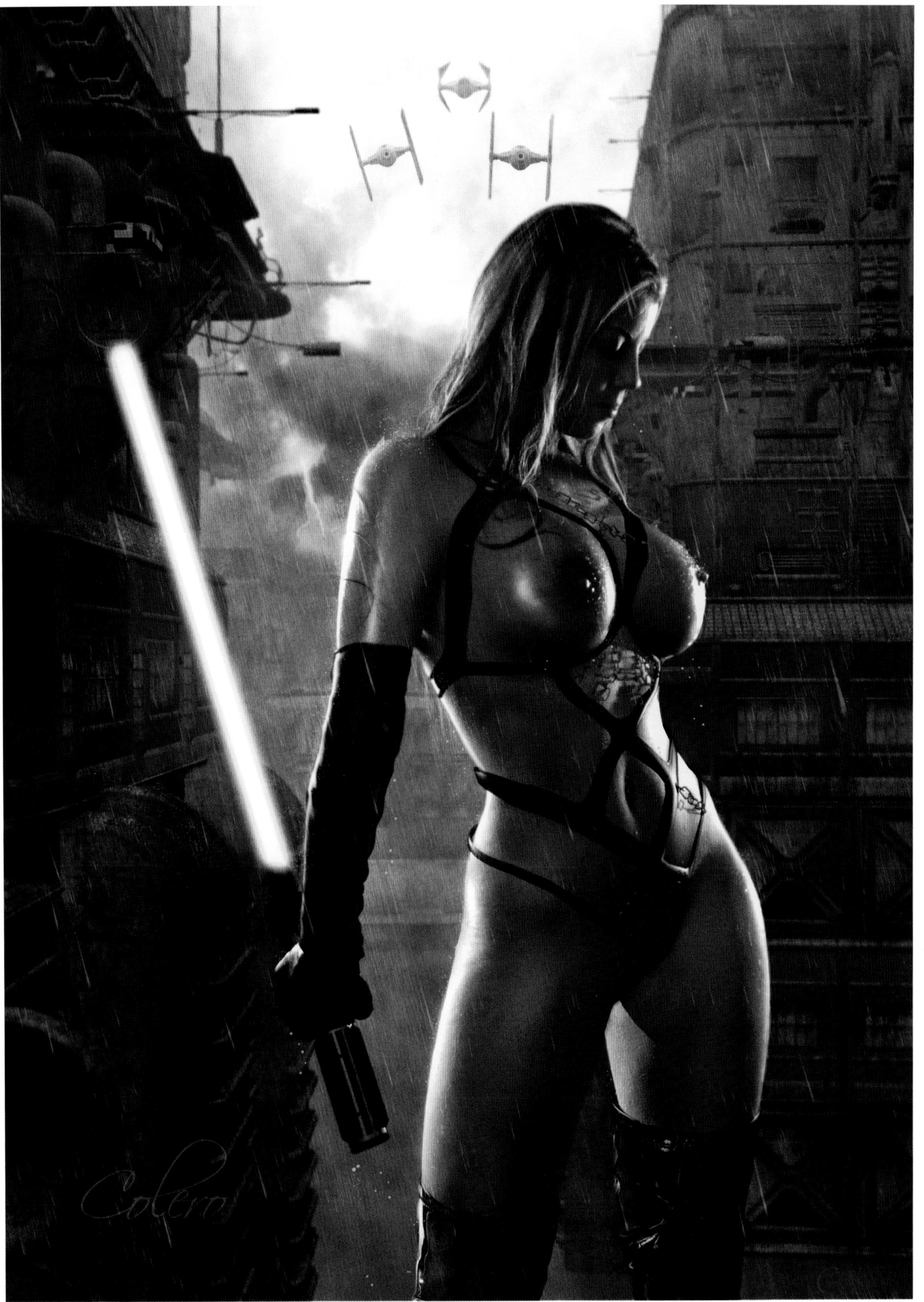

The Old Republic

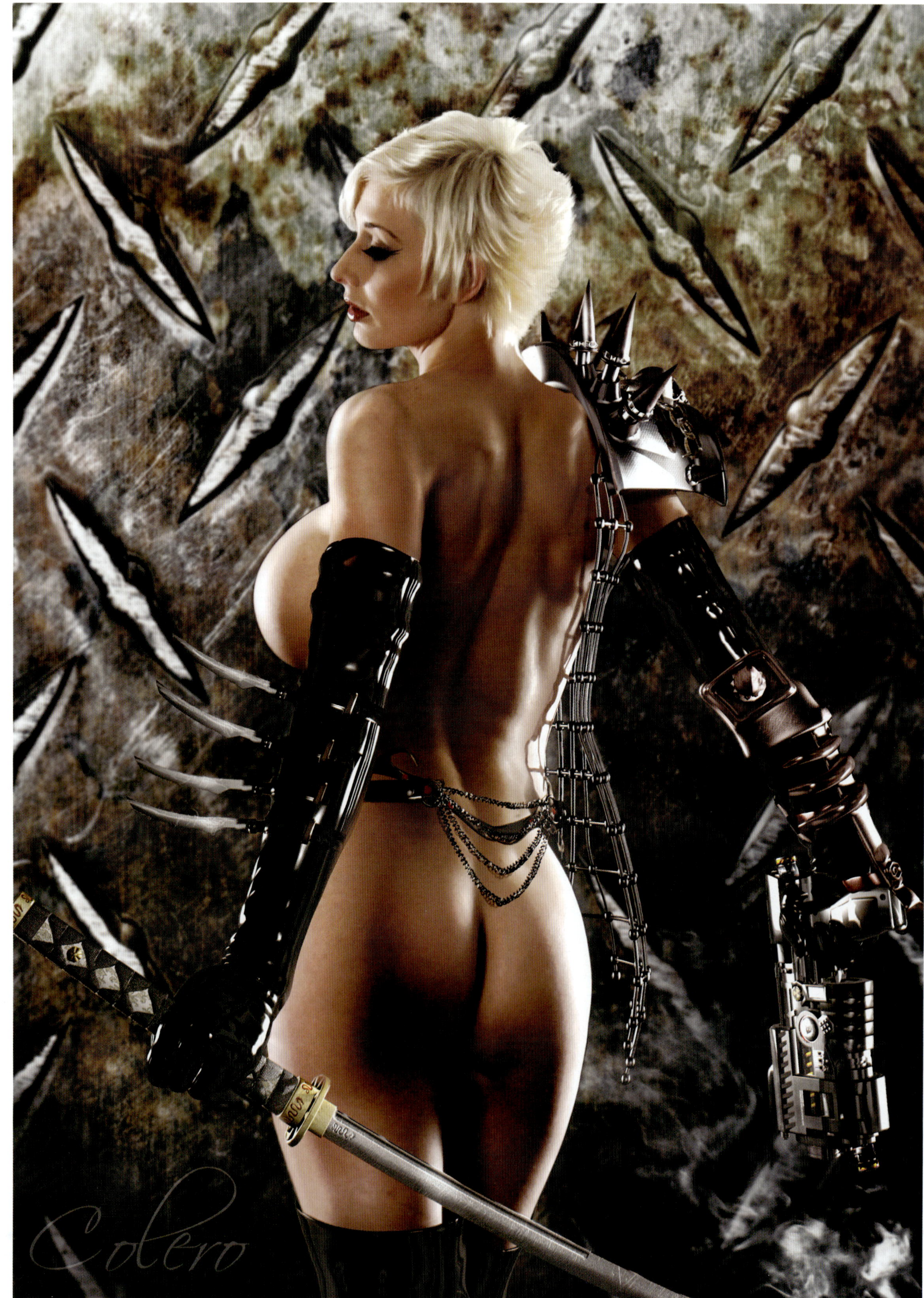

Dressed to Kill